COLLEGE Cooks™

SIMPLE INGREDIENTS, EASY RECIPES, GOOD TASTING FOOD

T.C. STEPHAN

Cool Eatz Publishing
Dana Point, California

College Cooks™

SIMPLE INGREDIENTS, EASY RECIPES, GOOD TASTING FOOD

T.C. STEPHAN

Published by:
Cool Eatz Publishing
Dana Point, California
Website: shopcollegecooks.com

Copyright © 2012 by T.C. Stephan

ISBN 978-0-9855617-0-3

Contributor: Nancy Bishop

Editors: Danielle Carlson; Robin Quinn, Quinn's Word for Word

Photographers: Marcus Tate, cover/back/food photos; Matt Sklar, b/w photos

Food Stylist: Debbie Castaldi

Cover and Book Designer: Peri Gabriel, Knockout Design, www.knockoutbooks.comn

Indexer: Katherine Stimson

For every book sold, $1 will be contributed to Feeding America®, at www.FeedingAmerica.org

Feeding America® provides low-income individuals and families with the fuel to survive and even thrive. As the nation's leading domestic hunger-relief charity, our network members supply food to 37 million Americans each year, including nearly 14 million children and nearly 3 million seniors. Serving the entire United States, more than 200 member food banks support more than 61,000 agencies that address hunger in all of its forms. For more information on how you can fight hunger in your community and across the country, visit www.FeedingAmerica.org.

CONTENTS

1

INTRODUCTION

College cooking? An oxymoron? Not anymore. With the plethora of cooking shows on TV and many celebrity chefs becoming as famous as professional athletes, college students across the country are taking a real interest in cooking.

My roommates and I are students at the University of Colorado at Boulder. Over the past three years of living together, we have perfected what to stock in our kitchen, how to shop for food on a budget, and how to get food on the table for two to four people.

In the following pages, you will find recommendations of what to stock in your kitchen cabinets, including basic condiments and spices, utensils, appliances (never go without an electric grill!), bakeware, and cookware. We have also outlined an initial shopping list to get you started, and added important sections on food preparation, safety, and storage.

Finally, we included our own favorite recipes that are quick to prepare, include limited ingredients, and are flavorful and healthy to eat. Some of these recipes are ones that we invented while experimenting in our kitchen, and others have been contributed by our friends and family. We even have a section detailing ten different ways to use a pre-roasted chicken.

We hope that you find our book useful in your quest to learn how to stock your kitchen, shop for food, prep ingredients, and cook delicious meals. Once you prepare these recipes, you will be ready for more complicated ones later, or you may find the inspiration to create your own. With these easy-to-read lists and simple recipes, you too can be as successful at cooking for yourself on a budget as we have been.

Turn the page and get started! You will not regret it.

Good luck!

— SIX GUYS IN BOULDER, COLORADO

Taylor Stephan, Cory and Kirk MacDonald,

Kevin Kotke, Andy Rovzar, and Alex McKee

2

TAYLOR'S STORY

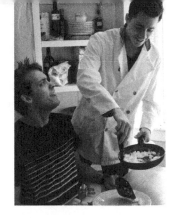

While other kids were watching cartoons and the Disney Channel, I spent my TV hours glued to the many Food Network programs that populated daytime television. This is how, at age eight, I first became interested in cooking. My cousin and I used to watch *Iron Chef* together, and my grandmother eventually bought me a sushi maker to feed my interest in cooking.

Fast forward to me as a 19-year-old college sophomore with five roommates. What were we going to cook in our small kitchen? Our electric grill came in handy and saved us from eating PB&Js every day. Having six chefs in the same kitchen was too crowded, so I took the lead when it came to grocery shopping for the group and preparing the food. With our conflicting schedules, we couldn't always cook at the same time, but we always tried to make time for group dinners. Slowly, my roommates became interested in food as well, and we watched various food shows on TV for the inspiration to devise our own creations.

Now it's our senior year, and our group has become a bit of an anomaly. Unlike many of our friends who live together but shop separately and rarely eat together, we have bought our food together for the last three years and continue to cook together. Our secret is that we stay with the basics and then get creative from there, and it has led to three years of tasty meals.

Good luck! I look forward to hearing your comments on Facebook.

— TAYLOR

PROFILES OF THE SIX
COLLEGE COOKS

TAYLOR

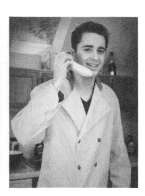

Age: 21

Hometown: Laguna Niguel, California

Favorite condiment: Likes his food *au naturel.*

Favorite food: Asian Stir-Fry Bowl

Favorite snack: Egg Drop Ramen

Contribution to dinner: Grill master

What he does for fun: Relaxing with buds/friends, listening to music, and playing intramural sports

KEVIN

Age: 21

Hometown: Newport Beach, California

Favorite condiments: Soy sauce, Sriracha hot sauce, and sour cream

Favorite food: Rice with butter and/or ketchup/Worcestershire sauce

Favorite snack: Quesadilla

Contribution to dinner: House sous chef

What he does for fun: Napping, board games, and playing intramural sports

CORY (Twin of Kirk)

Age: 22

Hometown: Newport Beach, California

Favorite condiment: A combination of ketchup and mayo that he calls "fancy sauce," which is really just his version of thousand island dressing

Favorite food: Cheeseburgers

Favorite snack: String cheese

Contribution to dinner: Makes the salads. Nickname is "Snackman."

What he does for fun: Board games, golf, lifting weights, and making movies

KIRK (Twin of Cory)

Age: 22

Hometown: Newport Beach, California

Favorite condiment: Honey mustard

Favorite food: Anything that is burnt; if it smells like smoke in the kitchen, it's Kirk who is cooking.

Favorite snack: Never snacks, only eats full meals.

Contribution to dinner: Big eater, cleans everyone else's plates.

What he does for fun: YouTube, watching movies, and procrastinating

ANDY

Age: 22

Hometown: Newport Beach, California

Favorite condiments: Butter, hazelnut spread, and salt

Favorite food: Chicken patty with extra cheese

Favorite snack: Waffle with hazelnut spread

Contribution to dinner: Makes anything with butter and side of salt.

What he does for fun: Lounging on the couch, watching classic movies, and eating cheese

ALEX

Age: 22

Hometown: Scottsdale, Arizona

Favorite condiment: Ranch dressing

Favorite food: Tuna salad

Favorite snack: PB&J waffle

Contribution to dinner: Called the "Sauce King."

What he does for fun: Making music, swimming, and nibbling on food, then leaving it around the house.

RECIPE KEY

 QUICK AND EASY:

Recipes that take less than 30 minutes to prep and cook

 BUDGET FRIENDLY:

Recipes that cost less than $10 to make

 HEALTHY:

Recipes that include vegetables, lean meats, fish, beans, eggs, whole wheat pasta, and/or grains

 VEGETARIAN:

Recipes that do not include meat, poultry, fish, game, or shellfish

 GOOD FOR LEFTOVERS:

Recipes that can be used to make more than one meal

BASICS OF
FOOD HANDLING

According to the USDA (www.fsis.usda.gov), the following information is important to safe food handling and preparation.

1. Always wash your hands thoroughly before handling food.

2. Raw meats should not be rinsed before cooking, as this can spread contamination.

3. Don't cross-contaminate! Keep raw meat away from other foods while you are prepping. Use different cutting boards for meat and for vegetables. After preparing raw meat, make sure to wash your hands, countertops, utensils, and cutting board with hot, soapy water.

THAWING FROZEN FOOD

You should never leave food on the countertop to thaw, as this could be dangerous.

Here are four methods for safe thawing:

✔ **Refrigerator:** Allows for slow thawing. This method usually requires you to put the food in the refrigerator the night before you are planning to cook.

✔ **Cold Water:** Seal food in a plastic bag and set in a bowl in the sink. Turn the faucet on and run cold water over the bag until the food is thawed. Do NOT use hot water, as this will start to cook the food.

✔ **Combination of Refrigerator and Cold Water:** This speeds up the process, rather than just using the frig.

✔ **Microwave:** Remove food from packaging before defrosting. **Place in a micro-wave-safe container or dish**. Select defrost or 30% power. Stop several times to flip the food. Cook immediately after thawing, as some parts of the food may be partially cooked.

COOKING MEAT SAFELY

✔ **Poultry:** All types of poultry should be cooked until well done and should never be pink on the inside. Internal temperature should be 165 degrees.

✔ **Raw Beef, Pork, Lamb, and Veal (steaks, chops and roasts with bone in):** These meats should have a minimum internal temperature of 145 degrees. According to the USDA, pork can now be eaten if pink inside or medium-well done.

✔ **Ground Meats like Pork, Beef, Lamb, and Veal: Ground meat** should always be cooked medium well to well-done. Internal temperature should be 160 degrees.

LEFTOVERS

✔ Throw away any food that has sat out longer than two hours, or one hour, if the air temperature is above 90 degrees.

✔ Place food in air-tight containers or plastic bags for refrigeration or freezing.

✔ Eat leftovers within four days.

COOKING WITH A MICROWAVE

Always use a microwave-safe container (glass is best).

✔ **Defrost:** Select defrost or set power to 30%, and stir food occasionally through-out the cycle.

✔ **Reheat:** You should usually reheat food at 70% power. To prevent splattering, cover with a paper towel or microwave-safe plastic wrap.

✔ **Cook:** Microwaves don't always cook food evenly, so we prefer to only use them to defrost or reheat. However, if you are in a hurry, you can use microwaves to prepare meals.

✔ **Microwave-Safe Cookware:** Any glass or heavy plastic container that says "microwave safe" is fine. Also, most paper plates, napkins, and paper towels are safe. NEVER put metal or aluminum foil in the microwave.

SO HOW LONG CAN I KEEP THAT?

Storage for Common Foods and When to Throw Them Away

✔ Do not buy food past the "sell by" or "use by" dates.

✔ Refrigerate perishable groceries within two hours, or one hour, if the air temperature is over 90 degrees.

1. **Eggs:** Three to five weeks in the refrigerator or on or before the expiration date. **Do not freeze eggs.** You can tell that eggs are no longer fresh if they float in a bowl of water.

2. **Deli Meat:** Three to five days in the refrigerator once package is opened. Two weeks in refrigerator unopened. **Do not freeze.**

3. **Mayonnaise:** Two months in refrigerator

4. **Hot Dogs:** One week in refrigerator once package is opened. Two weeks in refrigerator or 1-2 months in freezer unopened.

5. **Bacon:** Seven days in refrigerator. One month in freezer.

6. **Ground Beef, Turkey, Pork, Veal, or Lamb:** One to two days in refrigerator. Three to four months in freezer.

7. **Raw Steak or Lamb Chops:** Three to five days in refrigerator. Six to twelve months in freezer.

8. **Raw Chicken or Turkey Pieces:** One to two days in refrigerator. Nine months in freezer.

9. **Cooked Meat Leftovers:** Three to four days in refrigerator. Two to four months in freezer.

10. **Fresh Fish:** One to two days in refrigerator. Eight months in freezer.

11. **Pizza:** Three to four days in refrigerator. One to two months in freezer.

12. **Tomato Sauce:** Four to seven days in refrigerator

13. **Store-Bought Salsa:** Two weeks in refrigerator

14. **Milk:** Five days in refrigerator, or on or before expiration date. Sniff to see if it smells sour.

15. **Greens or Lettuce:** Five days in refrigerator

For frozen items, get a marker and date the plastic bags.
This is also helpful for open jars in the refrigerator.

MEASURING
CONVERSIONS

DRY MEASURING CONVERSIONS

1 cup	16 tbsp	48 tsp
3/4 cup	12 tbsp	36 tsp
2/3 cup	10-2/3 tbsp	32 tsp
1/2 cup	8 tbsp	24 tsp
1/3 cup	5-1/3 tbsp	16 tsp
1/4 cup	4 tbsp	12 tsp
1/8 cup	2 tbsp	6 tsp
1/16 cup	1 tbsp	3 tsp

LIQUID MEASURING CONVERSIONS

1 gallon	4 quarts	8 pints	16 cups
1/2 gallon	2 quarts	4 pints	8 cups
1/4 gallon	1 quart	2 pints	4 cups
1 cup	8 fl oz		
3/4 cup	6 fl oz		
2/3 cup	5-1/3 fl oz		
1/2 cup	4 fl oz		
1/3 cup	2-2/3 fl oz		
1/4 cup	2 fl oz		
1/8 cup	1 fl oz		
1/16 cup	1/2 fl oz		

7

KITCHEN ESSENTIALS

CONDIMENTS AND SPICES

1. Salt
2. Pepper
3. Red chili pepper flakes
4. Paprika
5. Italian seasoning
6. Mustard
7. Ketchup
8. Mayonnaise
9. Olive oil
10. Balsamic vinegar
11. Soy sauce
12. Chili-based hot sauce
13. Ranch dressing
14. Teriyaki sauce
15. Garlic powder
16. Sriracha hot sauce
17. Worcestershire sauce
18. White sugar
19. Brown sugar
20. Cinnamon
21. Flour

UTENSILS

1. Spatula
2. Wooden spoon
3. Timer
4. Set of measuring cups
5. Set of measuring spoons
6. Tongs
7. Colander
8. Two cutting boards—one for meat and one for vegetables
9. Cheese grater
10. Food thermometer
11. Six-inch strainer

APPLIANCES

1. Electric grill
2. Blender
3. Toaster oven
4. Rice cooker
5. Coffee maker
6. Microwave
7. Hand mixer
8. Can opener

BAKEWARE

1. Mixing bowls
2. Glass baking dishes (2 qt. and 4.8 qt. casserole)
3. Baking sheet
4. Jelly roll pan

COOKWARE

1. Pots: 2 qt., 4 qt., 8 qt.
2. Skillets: 8-inch and 10-inch

OTHER

1. Filtered water dispenser
2. Set of flatware
3. Drinking glasses
4. Dishes
5. Pitcher
6. Coffee mugs

KNIVES

1. Four-inch paring knife
2. Eight-inch Chef's knife
3. Serrated bread knife

MISCELLANEOUS

1. Plastic wrap
2. Foil
3. Freezer bags

COOKING
TERMINOLOGY

1. **Boiling:** Bringing a liquid (most likely water) to its highest temperature. Used for cooking potatoes, pasta, quinoa, and rice.

2. **Simmering:** Liquid is only slightly bubbling. Achieved by setting the temperature to low once the liquid is boiling. Used for sauces, soups, and chili.

3. **Steaming:** Using the steam from heated water to cook the food. Requires no oils. Used for cooking vegetables.

4. **Sautéing:** Cooking food in a small amount of oil over medium to high heat while regularly stirring food. Used to cook onions and vegetables. Wok works best.

5. **Grilling:** Cooking food on an electric grill or outdoor grill. Used to cook meat, fish, and vegetables.

6. **Scrambling:** Cooking eggs by continuously stirring and folding them in a hot pan until they set.

7. **Frying:** Cooking food in more fat (oil or butter), but at a lower temperature than sautéing. Used to cook fish, meat, and vegetables.

8. **Baking:** Cooking food in an oven set at a constant heat. Good for cooking roasts like beef and chicken, baked potatoes, fish, cakes, and casseroles.

9. **Broiling:** Cooking by using direct high heat under heating element. Good for steaks, lamb chops, chicken, and fish.

(from largest pieces to smallest)

✔ **Chop:** Cut food into smaller pieces.

✔ **Dice:** Cut food into tiny cubes.

✔ **Shred:** Cut food into narrow strips.

✔ **Grate:** Reduce food to threads using a grater.

✔ **Mince:** Cut food into pieces that are as small as possible.

DID YOU KNOW?

✔ **Acids:** Acids, like vinegar, tomatoes, limes, and lemons, are used to tenderize and marinate meats when added to oil.

✔ **Oil:** Oils, such as olive oil and canola oil, are fats like butter. All fats are not created equally. Olive oil is one of the best and healthiest for you.

✔ **Spices vs. Herbs:** Both spices and herbs are used to season dishes. Herbs come from leaves, while spices come from roots, tree bark, and seeds.

EXAMPLES OF SPICES

1. **Paprika:** Made from sweet peppers. Used for spice blends, potatoes, and fish. Mildest of the chilies.

2. **Chili Powder:** Made from a mixture of peppers, cumin, garlic, and oregano. Often used in Mexican food. Second hottest of the chilies.

3. **Cayenne Pepper:** Made from dried red chili peppers. Adds flavor and heat to soups and rubs. Hottest of the three chilies.

4. **Cinnamon:** Used in sweet dishes like apple pie and pumpkin pie.

5. **Cumin:** Golden in color. Often used in Mexican, Southwestern, and Middle Eastern cuisine.

6. **Garlic Powder:** Made from dehydrated garlic cloves. Not as strong as fresh minced garlic. Used in Italian, Mexican, and Asian cuisine.

EXAMPLES OF HERBS

1. **Basil:** Green leaves with a very strong aroma. Used in Italian food, such as pizza, pasta dishes, and pesto sauce.

2. **Oregano:** One of the most widely used herbs. Common in Mexican, Spanish, and Italian cuisine. Especially good in tomato sauce.

3. **Cilantro:** Pungent, fresh taste. Often used in Latin cuisine, particularly Mexican.

4. **Parsley:** Similar in appearance to cilantro, but with a milder flavor. Often used as a garnish or chopped up in marinades.

HOW TO SEASON WITH SALT

When we first started cooking, my roommates and I had a tendency to oversalt things. However, we found that since we like to use a lot of spices, we really don't need to oversalt our food. Here is our rule of thumb for salting foods:

✔ With pasta dishes, we use a big pinch of salt, which equates to about 1/8 tsp.

✔ For meats, including chicken, pork, beef, and lamb, we use 1/4-1/2 tsp of salt per pound. Then we can season to our taste by adding additional salt later.

There is nothing worse than when you take a big bite of your freshly cooked meal and all you can taste is salt. However, a little salt is important for bringing out the flavors in your food.

BUYING CUTS
OF MEATS

Since we are on a budget, we tend to use less expensive cuts of meat that are still full of flavor. They include the following:

- ✔ **Beef:** Our favorite cuts are round steak, skirt steak, and flank steak. We save the filet mignon and ribeye for when we are home visiting our parents.

- ✔ **Chicken:** We usually eat breasts or tenders. However, thighs, which are dark meat, are less expensive and don't dry out as easily as breasts.

- ✔ **Pork:** Less expensive than beef and with less fat. The pork tenderloin is very simple to cook.

- ✔ **Fish:** Tilapia, sole, red snapper, and cod are generally less expensive fish. Swordfish, wild salmon, and halibut are tasty fish that we eat when someone else is paying.

- ✔ **Lamb:** Loin chops and leg of lamb are usually less expensive than lamp rib chops.

10

INITIAL
SHOPPING LIST

This initial list should be enough to get you cooking right away. Look in your pantry and refrigerator, and cross off what you already have. Then go stock up!

Taylor's Tip

We find that since we are feeding three-plus guys in our house at any time, it's good to do our shopping at a bulk or club store like Costco or Sam's Club. Buying in bulk is especially efficient for frozen items and dry goods that can be stored for months.

PRODUCE

✔ Any fresh vegetables in season (e.g., broccoli, peppers, green beans, etc.)

✔ Any fresh fruits in season (e.g., pears, oranges, kiwis, etc.)

✔ Tomatoes   ✔ Bananas

✔ Lettuce   ✔ Carrots

✔ Avocados   ✔ Lemons

✔ Apples   ✔ Limes

REFRIGERATED/PERISHABLE ITEMS

✔ Fresh meat (chicken or beef)   ✔ Juice

✔ Rotisserie chicken   ✔ Hummus

✔ Hot dogs   ✔ Flour tortillas

✔ Eggs   ✔ Hamburger and hotdog buns

✔ Cheese (cheddar and jack)   ✔ Whole wheat sandwich bread

✔ Butter   ✔ English muffins

✔ Yogurt   ✔ Bagels

✔ Milk

FROZEN ITEMS

- ✔ Frozen shrimp
- ✔ Frozen hamburger
- ✔ Frozen ground turkey meat
- ✔ Frozen fish, individually wrapped
- ✔ Frozen chicken pieces
- ✔ Frozen vegetables for stir-fry
- ✔ Frozen pizza

DRY GOODS

- ✔ Canned albacore tuna
- ✔ Refried beans
- ✔ Bread crumbs/Panko (Japanese-style bread crumbs)
- ✔ Tortilla chips
- ✔ Granola bars
- ✔ Peanut butter
- ✔ Jelly
- ✔ Pancake/waffle mix (We like Bisquick.)
- ✔ Marinara sauce
- ✔ Nuts
- ✔ Mayonnaise
- ✔ Ketchup
- ✔ Apple cider vinegar
- ✔ Olive oil
- ✔ Mustard
- ✔ Soy sauce
- ✔ Sriracha sauce (Chinese hot sauce)

BREAKFAST

1. Preparing Eggs Like a Champ:
Hard-Boiled, Poached, Scrambled, Fried,
Sunny Side Up, and Omelets

2. Breakfast Burrito

3. Egg and Cheese Bagel

4. Loco Moco

5. Faux French Croissants with Ricotta Cheese
and Chocolate Chips

6. Blueberry and Banana Pancakes

7. Peanut Butter and Jelly Waffles

8. French Toast

9. Muesli and Yogurt

10. Smoothies

We have learned that, unlike learning to juggle eggs, learning to cook eggs means you will never go without dinner.

- **Hard-Boiled:** Fill a pot with water and place the eggs in the pot. Bring the water to a boil over high heat. Once the water boils, reduce the heat to low and let the eggs simmer for 10 minutes. Remove the eggs after 10 minutes, and then immediately immerse them in a separate bowl filled with cold water and ice. After 5 minutes, drain the water and refrigerate the eggs.

- **Poached:** Fill a pot with water and bring the fluid to a boil over high heat. Crack the egg and place its contents into a bowl. Next, carefully slip the egg into the pot of water so that it stays intact. Cook for approximately 2-1/2 minutes. Then, using a large spoon, carefully remove the egg from the boiling water, catching as much of it as possible.

- **Scrambled:** Scrambled eggs can be made with the yolks or without the yolks. Coat the bottom of a skillet with approximately 2 tsp of canola oil or butter. Warm the skillet over medium-low heat. While the skillet is heating, crack the eggs into a bowl and whisk together. (If you are only using the egg whites, two egg whites equal one whole egg.) Pour whisked eggs into the skillet and allow them to set for a minute. With a spatula, fold the eggs over while scraping the sides. Mix to allow larger pieces to break up, and turn the heat down so the eggs don't burn. Continue stirring until the eggs reach your desired dryness.

Separating the yolk from the white: Crack each egg in half and pour the yolk back and forth between each half of the shell while allowing the white to drain into a bowl below. For a simpler, yet messier method, you can pour the egg into your hand and allow the white portion to drain through your fingers into a bowl.

✔ **Fried:** Coat a skillet with 2 tsp of canola oil. Warm the skillet over medium-low heat. Gently crack the egg into the pan, using a spatula to stop the white from spreading out too much. Your egg should be roughly 4 inches in diameter as it cooks. After approximately 2 minutes, when the white part of the egg has set, gently flip the egg and continue cooking for another 2 minutes. You can adjust the cook time if you like a runnier yolk.

✔ **Sunny Side Up:** Coat a skillet with 2 tsp of canola oil. Warm the skillet over medium-low heat. Gently crack eggs into the skillet and cover it. After approximately 2-3 minutes, check the whites to see if they are firm and if the yolks have thickened. The center may be runny but should be at least 140 degrees. Remove from heat and serve.

✔ **Omelets:** Coat a skillet with 2 tsp canola oil and warm over medium-low heat. Crack the eggs into a bowl and whisk them together. Gently pour the eggs into the pan. Let the eggs set for 1-2 minutes. Run a spatula around the edge of the eggs to help release them from the pan. Carefully flip over the omelet in one piece and add cheese, sautéed vegetables, cooked meat, etc. Cook for 1-2 minutes more without burning. Take the pan off the heat and fold the omelet in half before serving.

Breakfast Burrito

SERVES 1

A jack-of-all-trades, this versatile winner can be eaten morning, noon, and night. It is best enjoyed at home or while you are running to class in your pajamas and robe. Muy bueno!

Ingredients

2 eggs or 4 egg whites

1/2 cup shredded cheddar cheese

2-3 tbsp canola oil or olive oil

1 (14.5 oz) can black beans

3 tbsp of your favorite salsa
(For home-made, see recipe p. 147.)

1 flour tortilla

Hot sauce (We like Cholula or Tapatio.)

Optional: Avocado, bacon, or leftover vegetables

Preparation

In a medium skillet, heat 1-1/2 tsp of canola oil or olive oil over medium-low heat. Pour the beans and salsa into the skillet. Stir and let simmer.

Taylor's Tip

Press the burrito in an electric grill (we like George Foreman's) to give it a toasty flavor.

Crack two eggs into a mixing bowl and whisk. In a separate small skillet, heat 3 tsp of oil on medium-low heat and add eggs. Let the eggs cook in the pan until they start to slightly firm up. Then fold eggs with a spatula to create large chunks. Right before taking the eggs off the burner, add the cheddar cheese. Cover and set aside.

Heat the flour tortilla in the microwave for 20 seconds on high. Remove and set on a plate. Top with bean mixture, eggs, and any optional ingredients. Fold tortilla, starting from one end, into a burrito. If you'd like, you can add your favorite hot sauce as you eat the burrito.

Burrito Enchilada Style

Pour 1/2 (10 oz) can of red enchilada sauce over the burrito, top with additional cheese, and place in a 350-degree pre-heated oven for 5 minutes.

Egg and Cheese Bagel

SERVES 1

A perfect grab-n-go item from our freshman days. It just takes a minute to scramble the eggs and add the cheese and any other toppings. Ah, to be young, fresh-faced, and without an embarrassing toga story.

Ingredients

2 eggs or 4 egg whites

Bagel of your choice, sliced in two

1 tbsp canola oil

1/2 cup shredded cheddar cheese or other cheese

1/8 tsp pepper

1/8 tsp salt

Optional: Tomato, lettuce, hot sauce

Preparation

Coat the bottom of a small skillet with canola oil, and warm over medium-low heat. Crack two eggs in a bowl and whisk together. When the oil is heated, pour in egg mixture. Let set for 1-2 minutes before mixing/folding with a spatula. Fold in cheese when eggs are almost done.

Meanwhile, toast the bagel slices in a toaster.

Spoon egg mixture onto toasted bagel and top with salt, pepper, and perhaps your favorite hot sauce, such as Tapitío or Cholula. Top with remaining bagel half to create a sandwich, slice in half again, and serve.

Loco Moco

SERVES 2

This traditional Hawaiian breakfast or plate lunch special is both tasty and filling. Just another reason why we fantasize about moving to Hawaii and buying a papaya grove when we graduate.

Ingredients

1/2 pound ground beef

1 cup white rice

2 cups water

2 eggs

2 tbsp canola oil

1/8 tsp pepper

1/8 tsp salt

Optional: 1 (14 oz) can of mushroom soup or gravy

Preparation

In a medium pot, bring 2 cups of water and 1 cup of rice to a boil. Lower heat and simmer covered for approximately 20 minutes, or until all the water has been absorbed. Set aside.

Pre-heat the electric grill. Form the ground beef into two 1/4-lb burger patties and season with salt and pepper. Place hamburger patties on the electric grill, and cook on each side for approximately 4-5 minutes. Meat should be cooked all the way through.

In a small skillet, heat canola oil over medium-low heat. Gently crack each egg into the skillet and let both set for approximately 2-3 minutes until the egg white is firm and the yolk has begun to harden. Flip the eggs over and continue cooking for another 2-3 minutes until all the white is cooked.

To assemble, scoop white rice into a shallow bowl, top with hamburger patty, and egg, and if you'd like, smother this in warm gravy or mushroom soup.

Note: If we are using a rice cooker, we use a 1:1 rice to water ratio. If we are using a pot on the stove, we use 2 cups water to 1 cup of rice.

Faux French Croissants with Ricotta Cheese and Chocolate Chips

SERVES 6

We all know that not all croissants are created equal. But when we want something almost as tasty and even flakier than the French original, we go for this low-cost, low-effort alternative. It hits the spot and beats getting up early for a flight to France before class. Since it's a crossover food, it can be served as a breakfast or as dessert at brunch, lunch, or dinner.

Ingredients

1 pastry dough roll (We prefer Pillsbury.)

1 small container of whole or part-skim ricotta cheese

1 cup chocolate chips

Optional: 1/2 cup fruit jam

Preparation

Pre-heat the oven to 350 degrees. Take out the dough from the container, and spread it out into small triangles on a small jelly roll pan.

Top each triangle with 2 tsp of ricotta cheese and 6-8 morsels of chocolate. If you are using jam, add 2 tsp of jam per triangle. Starting with the tip of the triangle, roll into a cylinder. Bake the croissants for 10-12 minutes until slightly brown on top.

Remove from the oven, let rest for 2-3 minutes, and serve.

Taylor's Tip

. . . .

To impress someone you're seeing, serve this as dessert on a date night, and tell your date that it's like you are having dinner in Paris.

Blueberry and Banana Pancakes

SERVES 2-4
(MAKES ABOUT A DOZEN PANCAKES)

*Since we often sleep through breakfast, brunch is our first
(and usually our favorite) meal. These tart and sweet pancakes are a
perfect way to start a weekend morning at 11 am.*

Ingredients

2 cups of pancake mix

1 egg

1 cup blueberries

1 banana, sliced

1 cup milk

2 tsp baking powder

2 tsp canola oil

Optional: powdered sugar, maple syrup, or jam

Preparation

In a medium bowl, combine pancake mix, egg, milk, and baking powder according to the directions on the box. Add blueberries and the sliced banana.

In a medium skillet, warm canola oil over medium-low heat. When the oil is crackling, add one ladle at a time of the batter. After about 1 minute, each pancake should start to bubble on top. Flip the pancakes over and cook for 1-2 more minutes until cooked all the way through.

Serve with powdered sugar, maple syrup, or jam.

Taylor's Tip

*Baking powder
makes them lighter
than a feather!*

Peanut Butter and Jelly Waffles

SERVES 1

When we have nothing left in the fridge besides ketchup and pickles, we pull out our frozen waffles to save the day.

Ingredients

2 waffles

2 tbsp peanut butter

2 tbsp jelly

Preparation

Toast both waffles and then spread on peanut butter and jelly. Cut in half and serve.

Taylor's Tip

· · · · · · · · · · · · ·

Try hazelnut spread (we like Nutella) instead of peanut butter and jelly.

French Toast

SERVES 1

The French gave us French fries, the Statue of Liberty, and the freedom to eat
snails. They also gave us French toast.

Ingredients

Two slices white bread or bread of choice

2 eggs

1 cup milk

1/2 cup cereal of choice (We like Honey Bunches of Oats or Corn Flakes.)

1 tbsp of butter

1 tsp granulated sugar

1 tsp vanilla extract

1/4 tsp cinnamon

Maple syrup to taste

Powdered sugar to taste

Preparation

In a shallow bowl, mix eggs, vanilla, and milk. Pour cereal into a separate bowl. Dip two pieces of bread into the egg mixture and soak on each side. Then dip soaked bread into the cereal to coat evenly

In a medium skillet, warm butter over medium-low heat. When melted, add the two slices of bread. After approximately 1-2 minutes, flip bread. Bread should be browned but not burnt. Continue cooking for another 1-2 minutes. Sprinkle with cinnamon and granulated sugar just before removing the pan from the burner.

Serve with syrup and powdered sugar.

Muesli and Yogurt

SERVES 1

We think this is a great way to start the morning. The mixture of oats, nuts, fruit, and yogurt is not only tasty, but it's also filling enough to last us until we make lunch—or if we're out of groceries, until we head next door and raid our neighbor's fridge.

Ingredients

1 cup muesli cereal

3 tbsp Greek style yogurt

1-1/2 cups milk

1/4 cup raisins

1/2 tsp cinnamon

1/4 tsp vanilla

Optional: sugar, berries, banana

Preparation

In small bowl, add muesli, yogurt, milk, raisins, cinnamon, and vanilla. Mix and let set in the refrigerator for at least one hour. When you are ready to eat, sweeten the dish with sugar or additional cinnamon. Top with banana slices or berries.

Smoothies

S E R V E S   2

Thicker than juice, but easier to eat with a straw than fruit salad,
a smoothie is our favorite way to get our daily serving of fruit.
We drink these any time of day, and even freeze them into
popsicles for a refreshing summer treat!

Hawaiian Smoothie / Ingredients

1 banana, peeled

1 cup of juice, including guava, pineapple, orange, or coconut water

3/4 cup frozen mango pieces

3/4 cup frozen papaya pieces

1/2 cup frozen strawberry pieces

Water, if needed

Berry Smoothie / Ingredients

1 banana, peeled

1 cup apple juice

3/4 cup frozen raspberry pieces

3/4 cup frozen blueberry pieces

1/2 cup frozen strawberry pieces

Water, if needed

Preparation

Put all ingredients in a blender and blend until smooth. For added thickness, use less juice. To thin out, add water.

> **Note:** *If you are using fresh fruit, add ice.*
> *If you are using frozen fruit, no ice is required.*

Taylor's Tip

· · · · · · · · · · · · · ·

I like to add protein
powder to make it a
complete meal and
yogurt or ice cream
for added flavor.

SANDWICHES

1. We like both hot and cold sandwiches, depending on our moods. When we're craving something hot and toasty, we grill it on an electric grill (we like George Foreman's) with these easy steps:

   a. *Plug in the electric grill or Panini press.*

   b. *Allow it to heat until the red light goes off.*

   c. *Clean and then prep the grill with olive oil spray or olive oil.*

   d. *Prepare your sandwich with everything on it, place on grill, and close the lid.*

   e. *Grill for a few minutes on each side.*

2. For an added treat, use your favorite baguette, focaccia bread, or wheat or sourdough.

3. Instead of lettuce, use sprouts or cabbage.

4. Rather than tomatoes, use roasted red peppers from a jar or peperoncini.

5. For sandwiches, it is always good to keep mustard, ketchup, and mayonnaise on hand. For additional flavor, we like hummus, an aioli spread, pesto, and even guacamole. All of these spreads can be bought pre-made at the local grocery store or you can make them yourself.

Peanut Butter, Banana, and Honey on Toast

SERVES 1

This is comfort food that we loved as children, and even though we're currently working on being adults, it's still fun to eat like a kid sometimes.

Ingredients

2 tbsp of peanut butter

1/2 banana, sliced

1 tbsp of honey

1 piece of bread

Preparation

Toast the bread. Coat the bread with peanut butter and honey, and top with the sliced banana.

Egg Salad Sandwich

SERVES 1

*This became one of our favorite sandwiches after we graduated
from scrambling eggs to hard-boiling them. Put off studying for finals
and try this test instead.*

Ingredients

2 eggs

2 tsp mustard

1 tbsp mayonnaise

2 slices bread of choice

1 slice of tomato

1 lettuce leaf

Pinch of salt and pepper

Preparation

Fill a pot with water and place the eggs in the pot. Bring water to a boil over high heat. Reduce heat to low and let eggs simmer for 10 minutes. Remove eggs after 10 minutes, and immediately immerse them in a separate bowl filled with cold water and ice. After 5 minutes, drain the water.

To peel the eggs, roll them on the counter with your hand using light pressure so that the shell cracks. Then peel away the shells. Once peeled, use a fork to break up the eggs in a bowl. Mix in mustard and mayonnaise, and add salt and pepper.

Spread on your bread of choice and top with lettuce and tomato. You can also toast your bread first, for a crunchy counterpart to the egg salad.

Mozzarella, Tomato, and Arugula Sandwich

SERVES 1

This sandwich is super fresh and very flavorful. The heartiness of the cheese and tomatoes makes us forget that there is no meat on this!

Ingredients

3 thick slices of mozzarella cheese

1 tomato, thickly sliced

1/2 cup of arugula, packed

1 tbsp olive oil or pesto sauce (recipe p. 153)

Freshly ground pepper

French roll

Preparation

Slice the French roll in half lengthwise. Coat the inside of each piece of bread with olive oil and pile on cheese, tomato, and arugula. Season with pepper.

Classic BLT

SERVES 1

The combination of Bacon, Lettuce, and Tomato as BLT has been around a long time. We tried a few different combinations to see if we could improve it (Butterscotch, Linguini, and Turkey or Beef jerky, Lasagna, and Tortilla chips), but the original is still the best.

Ingredients

5 slices of bacon

1 small tomato, sliced

2 lettuce leaves

1 tsp mayonnaise

2 slices of sourdough bread

Optional: avocado, sliced

Preparation

Pre-heat oven to 375 degrees. For less fat, bake the bacon for 15 minutes on a rack with a pan underneath to catch the drippings. The bacon can also be microwaved according to the directions on the package.

Meanwhile, toast the bread to your liking. Once the bacon is cooked, assemble the sandwich starting with spreading the mayonnaise on the toasted bread, and then adding the bacon, lettuce, tomato, and optional avocado.

Grilled Cheese

S E R V E S 1

We all agree that this is a sandwich we never get tired of, and it's especially tasty when we've just gotten back from snowboarding.

Ingredients

4 slices of cheese total, jack and cheddar

2 slices of sourdough bread

1 tbsp butter

Preparation

Coat one side of each slice of bread with butter. Heat a small skillet on medium heat. Lay one slice of bread in the pan butter-side down. Add the slices of cheese, and then top the cheese with the other piece of bread, butter-side up, to form a sandwich. Cook on each side until the bread is slightly browned and the cheese is melted.

Serve hot.

Easy Tuna Melt Variation

A grilled cheese can be made into an easy tuna melt by simply adding tuna between the layers of cheese. To make one, mix a drained can of albacore tuna in water with 2 tbsp of mayonnaise. After laying your buttered slice of bread in the pan, top with half the cheese, a large scoop of tuna, the remaining cheese, and then the second slice of bread butter-side up. Heat on each side until the bread is slightly browned, the tuna is warm, and the cheese is melted.

Serve hot.

Note: An electric grill can be used instead of the skillet.

Tuna and Olive Oil

SERVES 1

Tuna packed in olive oil is the sophisticated older brother of tuna packed in water. It's the same tuna, but the olive oil gives it a richer flavor. I learned to love tuna in olive oil after I studied abroad in Spain.

Ingredients

1 (5 oz) can of tuna in olive oil, undrained

1/8 tsp black pepper

1/8 tsp garlic salt

2 slices of sourdough bread

Optional: chopped peperoncini or chopped celery

Preparation

Start toasting your bread. Meanwhile, in a medium bowl, mix together all the remaining ingredients. Top the toasted bread with the tuna mixture, and add the remaining piece of bread.

Turkey and Pepper Jack Cheese Wrap

SERVES 1

Sometimes it's just a tortilla kind of day. And sometimes we are just out of bread.

Ingredients

1 flour tortilla

2 slices of pepper jack cheese

3 slices of deli turkey breast

Mustard or mayonnaise

Optional: lettuce, tomato

Preparation

Warm the tortilla in a skillet over low heat. Once warm, remove from heat and spread a squeeze of mustard or mayonnaise evenly over the tortilla. Place turkey, cheese, lettuce, and tomato toward one side of the wrap. Fold into a wrap starting with end that is lined with ingredients.

Taylor's Tip

. . . .

For added variation, I like to use spinach wraps, and when I'm on a health kick, I go for whole-wheat wraps. They are all delicious!

Roast Beef and Cheddar with Honey Mustard

SERVES 1

They say beef is what's for dinner, but in our house, it's for lunch. It's also sometimes for a midnight snack when all we have are cold cuts.

Ingredients

4 slices of roast beef

3 slices of cheddar cheese

2 tbsp of spicy mustard

1 tsp of honey

2 slices of sourdough or wheat bread

Optional: lettuce, tomato

Preparation

Mix the mustard and honey in a small bowl until combined. Apply to one side of two pieces of bread. Fill the sandwich with roast beef, cheddar cheese, and any optional toppings.

Croque Monsieur and Croque Madame

(AKA HAM AND CHEESE)

SERVES 1

*Voila! The French version of ham and cheese. For added authenticity,
you can serve it in a beret instead of on a plate.*

Ingredients

2 slices of Swiss or Gruyère cheese (Swiss is the cheaper option.)

3 slices of smoked ham

2 tsp butter

2 slices of sourdough or wheat bread

Optional: 1 egg, 1 tsp canola oil, pinch of salt and pepper

Preparation

Pre-heat your electric grill. Butter one side of the bread, and lay the bread butter-side down on the grill. Layer it with cheese and ham slices, and top the sandwich with the remaining slice of buttered bread with the butter-side up.

Close electric grill lid, and grill for 2-3 minutes on each side until the bread is golden brown and the cheese is melted.

Serve hot.

To make a **Croque Madame**:

Top the sandwich with a Sunny Side Up Egg (recipe p. 40) seasoned with salt and pepper.

Pastrami Quesadilla
with Aioli Sauce

SERVES 1

Whose says quesadillas should only be part of Mexican cuisine?
We like to think of this as fusion fare.

Ingredients

1 flour tortilla

1 tsp olive oil

2 slices of jack cheese

2 slices of pastrami

2-3 tsp of aioli sauce (recipe p. 148)

Optional: spicy sauce

Preparation

Warm olive oil over low to medium heat. Add the flour tortilla and layer the cheese and pastrami slices. Drizzle aioli sauce on the cheese and meat before folding the tortilla in half.

Press down on the folded tortilla with a spatula, and turn after 1-2 minutes or when the cheese is melting. Cook for another 1-2 minutes and then remove from heat.

Serve hot. Top with your favorite spicy sauce. Our favorites are Tapatío, Sriracha, and Cholula.

Taylor's Tip
· · · · · · · · · · · · · ·

*Aioli is basically
a fancy version of
mayonnaise. I like it
because I can make
it any flavor I want.
Garlic tends to be my
go-to, except for on
date night when
I am worried about
my breath!*

Cuban Style Sandwich

SERVES 1

We call this sandwich "Cuban style" because it's not quite a Cubano without pork. Unless you are a celebrity chef, you probably don't have roasted pork in your fridge. Luckily, this one is simpler to make and equally as tasty.

Ingredients

French roll, pita bread, or Italian bread

3 slices of smoked ham or pulled pork (See p. 104 for recipe, Korean Pork Tenderloin.)

2 Swiss cheese slices

2-3 tsp yellow mustard

Pickles, sliced thin

Peperoncini

Preparation

Slice roll or pita in half and fill with ham, cheese, mustard, pickles and peperoncini. Grill on electric grill until grill marks form and cheese starts to melt.

Serve hot.

Pulled Chicken Sandwich

SERVES 1

*We all love sloppy joes, so we decided to take it to the next level
by using pulled chicken from chicken thighs instead of ground beef.
These are also less sloppy, so you have a better chance of
keeping your shirt and your face sauce-free!*

Ingredients

1-2 chicken thighs, skin off and shredded off bone after cooking

1 tbsp sweet chili sauce

Juice of 1 small lemon

4 springs of cilantro, chopped

Pinch of salt and black pepper

2 slices of sour dough bread

2 slices of jack cheese

Half tomato, sliced

2 tsp butter

Olive oil spray (We like PAM's.)

Preparation

Heat electric grill on medium-high. Coat with an olive oil spray.

Mix the sweet chili sauce, lemon juice, cilantro, salt, and pepper, and apply to the chicken thighs. Cook the thighs on the electric grill for approximately 12-15 minutes in total, splitting equal time on both sides. Set aside to rest. Once cooled, shred chicken from bone and set aside.

Butter one side of each slice of sourdough bread. Add shredded chicken to non-buttered side of one slice, top with cheese and tomato slices, add second slice with buttered side on top, and heat on a clean electric grill on medium for 2-3 minutes on each side.

Serve hot.

Tailgate Sausage Sandwich

SERVES 6

*As college guys, we tailgate pretty often. So, to change it up,
we grab some fully cooked sausages instead of hotdogs and throw them
on the grill. Any sausage variety works with this recipe,
so try a new one every time!*

Ingredients

6 fully cooked sausages

Olive oil spray (We like PAM's.) or
1 tbsp olive oil

Hot dog buns

Chimichurri sauce (recipe p. 156)

Preparation

Pre-heat an electric grill and coat with olive oil. Add sausages and grill for approximately 5 minutes each side. Place in bun and top with chimichurri sauce and any other condiments.

SALADS

13

We always have a variety of greens around, including mixed greens, romaine, green leaf, red leaf, iceburg, or butter lettuces. You can find prepared lettuce in bags at the grocery store or at the box or club stores (we prefer Costco).

The dressings you use will depend on the heartiness of the lettuce. With mixed greens, always use a lighter dressing like a vinaigrette. With heartier lettuce (stronger leaves), like green leaf or romaine, you can use ranch or any cream-based dressing.

Below we have a list of salad ingredients to help you create your own salad. Just choose one or more ingredients from each category. Get creative! There are almost no bad combinations.

STEP 1: PICK A LETTUCE

- ✔ Green leaf
- ✔ Iceberg
- ✔ Red leaf
- ✔ Romaine
- ✔ Butter lettuce
- ✔ Mixed greens/spring mix

STEP 2: ADD VEGETABLES

- ✔ Shredded carrots
- ✔ Chopped tomato
- ✔ Sliced cucumber
- ✔ Sliced avocados
- ✔ Garbanzo beans
- ✔ Chopped red onion or green onion

STEP 3: ADD CRUNCH

- ✔ Almonds
- ✔ Pine nuts
- ✔ Pistachios
- ✔ Tortilla chips, broken
- ✔ Ramen noodles, broken
- ✔ Croutons

STEP 4: ADD SALTY FLAVOR

- ✔ Salami
- ✔ Feta cheese
- ✔ Bacon bits

STEP 5: ADD PROTEIN

- ✔ Cooked shrimp
- ✔ Shredded chicken
- ✔ Hard-boiled eggs

STEP 6:   ADD SWEETNESS

✔ Dried cranberries   ✔ Apple slices

STEP 7:   CHOOSE A DRESSING

(Store bought or home-made)

✔ Caesar   ✔ Ranch

✔ Vinaigrette   ✔ Balsamic Vinaigrette

✔ Asian

(See Basic Salad Dressings chapter, pp. 142 to 143,
for all of these dressing recipes.)

Basic Green Salad

SERVES 2-4

Ingredients

1 head green leaf lettuce or iceberg torn into bite-sized pieces

1 cucumber, sliced

Croutons

Dressing suggestion: Ranch or Balsamic Vinaigrette (recipes p. 143 and p. 142)

Preparation

In a colander, wash lettuce and pat dry with paper towel. In a bowl, toss lettuce with cucumber, croutons and dressing.

Mixed Green Salad

SERVES 2-4

Ingredients

1 bag of mixed spring baby lettuce

Feta cheese

Slivered almonds

Dressing suggestion: Vinaigrette (recipe p. 142)

Preparation

In a colander, rinse and pat dry the lettuce leaves. In a bowl, toss lettuce, crumbled feta, and slivered almonds with dressing.

Caesar Salad

SERVES 2-4

Ingredients

1 head romaine lettuce

Parmesan cheese, shaved

Croutons

Caesar dressing (recipe p. 142)

Preparation

Cut romaine lettuce width-wise into 2 inch strips. Rinse in a colander and pat dry with paper towel. In a bowl, toss lettuce and shaved Parmesan with dressing. Top with croutons.

Chinese Chicken Salad

SERVES 2-4

Ingredients

1 head romaine lettuce, torn into bite-sized pieces

1 packet of ramen noodles

1 cup almond slivers or pine nuts

2 cups chopped, cooked chicken

1 (11 oz) can of mandarin orange or tangerine slices

Asian Vinaigrette dressing (recipe p. 143)

Optional: sunflower seeds, cilantro, and/or chopped green onions

Preparation

Cut romaine lettuce width-wise into 2 inch strips. In a colander, rinse lettuce and pat it dry with paper towels. In a large bowl, toss lettuce with remaining ingredients and Asian Vinaigrette dressing.

College Cooks™

Tomato and Mozzarella Salad

SERVES 2

When we are out of lettuce, we substitute this flavorful dish instead
of a salad. It's like an Italian caprese salad!

Ingredients

3 medium-sized tomatoes, sliced, or a
pint of grape tomatoes

1 small container of marinated
mozzarella balls

6 fresh basil leaves, chopped

Optional: olive oil to sprinkle over salad;
pepper.

Preparation

In a large bowl, mix together tomatoes, mozzarella, and basil.

Serve cold.

SOUPS

14

There is nothing like home-made, hearty soups. We have our favorites depending on our schedule and mood, and we'd like you to find your favorites as well. Since we live in a state with four seasons, we never get tired of spreading these soup recipes throughout all four.

Vegetable Barley Soup

SERVES 4-6

*This filling soup is a great, warm meal on a cold, wintry day
or a great, healthy meal on a day in which we each ate
four servings of French toast for breakfast.*

Ingredients

1 medium onion, diced

3 carrots, chopped in 1/2 inch pieces

3 celery stalks, chopped in 1/2 inch pieces

3 cloves garlic, minced

1 (14.5 oz) can of diced tomatoes

4 tbsp olive oil

2/3 cup brown lentils

2/3 cup barley

1 (32 oz) box of chicken broth or vegetable broth

1-1/2 cups of water

1/8 tsp pepper

1/8 tsp salt

Parmesan cheese

Preparation

In a large pot, warm the olive oil over medium-low heat. Add garlic and sauté for 2 minutes. Add celery and carrots, and continue sautéing for an additional 2 minutes.

Add the remaining ingredients (except the cheese) and bring to a boil. Lower heat and simmer for at least an hour. Add additional water for a thinner broth.

Ladle into bowls and top with Parmesan cheese. Serve hot.

Creamy Tomato Basil Soup

SERVES 2-4

This creamy, tasty soup pairs perfectly with our grilled cheese.
It's a fitting meal for a cold night.

Ingredients

3 tbsp olive oil

1 large onion, chopped

2 (32 oz) cans of diced tomatoes

2 garlic cloves, minced

1 (32 oz) box of vegetable or chicken stock

1 cup of water

2 tbsp tomato paste

3 tbsp shredded fresh basil leaves

2/3 cup heavy cream (optional but necessary for creaminess)

1/2 tsp salt

Preparation

In a large pot, heat olive oil on medium-low heat. Add garlic and onion. Sauté until onions are translucent, approximately 5 minutes.

Add tomatoes, stock, water, tomato paste, and salt, and bring to a boil. Lower heat and simmer for 20 minutes, stirring occasionally.

Pour mixture into blender and add shredded basil. Blend until smooth. Return soup mixture to the pot and add cream. Heat on medium-low, until warm but not boiling.

Serve hot.

Pasta and Bean Soup

SERVES 4

A great combination of pasta and beans for a nutritious, hearty soup.

Ingredients

2 cups of small pasta shells

2 celery stalks, chopped in 1/2 inch pieces

3 tbsp olive oil

1 small onion, diced

2 large carrots, chopped in 1/2 inch pieces

2 cups chicken broth or vegetable broth

1 (14.5 oz) can of diced tomatoes

1 (15 oz) can cannellini beans, rinsed
and drained

2 cups of water

1 tbsp chopped fresh basil

1 tsp cayenne pepper

1/8 tsp salt

1/8 tsp pepper

Red chili pepper flakes

Parmesan cheese

Preparation

Fill a medium pot halfway with water. Cook pasta according to the instructions on the box.

Warm the olive oil in a medium pot over medium-low heat. Add celery, onion, and carrots, and sauté for 5 minutes until vegetables are tender. Add broth, tomatoes with juice, cayenne pepper, cannellini beans, salt, pepper, and water. Cover and bring to a boil, then lower heat and simmer for 1 hour. Stir in cooked pasta.

Ladle soup into bowls and top with Parmesan cheese, chopped basil and red chili pepper flakes. Serve hot.

Gran's Chicken Noodle Soup

SERVES 4-6

*This recipe was passed down from my grandmother to my mother
and now to me. And even though it's been around a long time, we never get
tired of it—just like my grandmother!*

Ingredients

3 chicken breasts, skin on, bone in

5 large carrots, chopped in 1 inch pieces

4 celery stalks, chopped in 1 inch pieces

1 bag of thin egg noodles

1/2 tsp of salt

12 cups water

Pinch of pepper

Preparation

Fill a large pot with 12 cups of water. Place chicken breasts in water and bring to a boil. Lower heat and simmer for 10 minutes. Use a small strainer to skim off chicken residue from the top of the water.

Add carrots, celery, pepper, and salt. Bring to a boil and then lower heat and simmer for at least an hour and half.

Turn off heat temporarily. Remove chicken and separate chicken meat from the bone. Strain broth into a large bowl to catch any potential bones.

Return chicken and broth to the original pot and bring to a boil again. Add the amount of noodles you like and cook according to the instructions on the bag.

Serve hot.

Game Day Chili

SERVES 4-6

This chili is always a hit at our tailgate parties. It's very easy to make if you have a can opener. Otherwise, you may spend the day trying to open the cans with your teeth and end up missing the game.

Ingredients

1 pound of ground turkey meat (Leave out for vegetarian chili.)

1 (32 oz) can of chili beans

1 (15 oz) can kidney beans

1 (15 oz) can of northern white beans

1 (32 oz) can of crushed tomatoes

1 (15 oz) can of stewed tomatoes

4 small (5.5 oz) cans tomato juice

1 green pepper, diced

1 large onion, diced

2 garlic cloves, minced

1 cup frozen corn

1 cup of water

3 tbsp of olive oil

1 tbsp red chili pepper flakes

1 tbsp chili powder

1 tsp cumin

2 bay leaves

Cheddar cheese, grated

Dollop of sour cream

1 bunch of green onions, chopped

Preparation

In a large pot, warm olive oil on medium-low heat, add garlic, and sauté for 2 minutes. Add the diced onion and green pepper, and continue to sauté until the onion is translucent. Increase the heat to medium, add turkey, and cook, stirring regularly, until the meat is only slightly pink.

Add the remaining ingredients (except cheese, sour cream, and chopped green onions), increase the heat to high, and bring to a boil. Cover pot and simmer over low heat for at least 1 hour.

Top with grated cheddar cheese, sour cream, and chopped green onions. Serve hot.

PASTAS

1. Grazie Italy!

2. Spaghetti Marinara with Veggies

3. Bow Tie Pasta with Pesto and Pine Nuts

4. Baked Ziti

5. Creamy Mac 'n' Cheese

6. Vegetarian Lasagna

7. Risotto

8. Penne with Tomatoes, Olives, and Artichoke Hearts

9. Ravioli with Shrimp

10. Spicy Shrimp Pasta with Tomatoes and Garlic

11. Penne with Tuna, Tomatoes, Garlic, and Capers

There is a common theme throughout many of our pastas of including red tomatoes and garlic. We have added some other colors, including Green Basil Pesto and yellow Mac 'n' Cheese. Add the spaghetti, and we have incorporated the three colors of the Italian flag, red, green and white—which is only fitting for our pasta recipes. We have featured some staples like Lasagna (you can make this vegetarian or with meat sauce) and Baked Ziti as well.

Spaghetti Marinara with Veggies

SERVES 4

*If you are tired of using sauce from a jar, this recipe will help you
make the transition from store-bought sauce to home-made sauce—
otherwise known as liquid gold.*

Ingredients

1 lb spaghetti

3 garlic cloves, minced

4 tbsp olive oil

1 zucchini, chopped in 1 inch pieces

2 carrots, chopped in 1/2 inch pieces

2 celery stalks, chopped in 1/2 inch pieces

1 medium onion, diced

2 (14.5 oz) cans of crushed tomatoes

1 green bell pepper, chopped in 1 inch pieces

1 tbsp of oregano or Italian seasoning

2 bay leaves

1/4 tsp salt

1/4 tsp pepper

1 cup Parmesan cheese, grated

Optional: water

Preparation

Warm 4 tbsp of olive oil in a large pot on medium-low heat. Add onion, garlic, carrots, and celery. Sauté until onions are translucent, about 5 minutes.

Add crushed tomatoes, bay leaves, Italian seasoning, salt and pepper. Add water if the mixture is too thick.

Bring to a boil and then reduce heat to low and simmer. After 45 minutes, add zucchini and green bell pepper to the pot and continue simmering for 15 minutes.

Serve hot over your favorite spaghetti. Top with Parmesan cheese.

Bow Tie Pasta with Pesto and Pine Nuts

SERVES 4

This is one of our favorite dishes, and the green pesto sauce makes it especially festive for St. Patrick's Day.

Ingredients

1 lb of bow tie pasta

1 (7 oz) container of pesto sauce
(For home-made, see recipe p. 153.)

1/2 cup of pine nuts

Parmesan cheese, grated

Red chili pepper flakes

Optional: leftover chicken, chopped in
1 inch pieces

Preparation

Fill a large pot half of the way full with water and bring to a boil. Add pasta and cook according to the directions on the box. When cooked, drain in a colander and return to the pot.

Add your desired amount of pesto sauce and pine nuts, and mix. Top with grated Parmesan cheese and red chili pepper flakes. You can also add leftover chicken chopped into 1 inch pieces.

Serve hot.

College Cooks

Baked Ziti

This dish is Italian comfort food at its best. You usually can't go wrong
with a dish that uses two different cheeses!

Ingredients

1 lb ziti or penne pasta

1 tsp olive oil

6 garlic cloves, chopped

1/4 tsp red chili pepper flakes

1 (28 oz) can crushed tomatoes

3 cups of water

1/2 cup heavy cream

1/2 cup Parmesan cheese, grated

1/4 cup fresh basil, chopped

1 cup mozzarella cheese, grated

1/4 tsp salt

1/4 tsp pepper

Optional: sausage

Preparation

Pre-heat oven to 475 degrees.

In a large pan, warm olive oil over low to medium heat. Add garlic and red chili pepper flakes, and sauté for about 1 minute. Add crushed tomatoes, water, ziti, salt, and pepper. Cover and cook, stirring often. Adjust heat to maintain a simmer. Cook until ziti is tender, about 15 minutes.

Remove from heat, and stir in cream, Parmesan cheese, basil, and sausage (optional). Transfer mixture to an oven-safe glass dish (we like Pyrex). Sprinkle mozzarella evenly on top of the pasta and transfer to the pre-heated oven. Bake until the cheese has melted and browned on top, about 10 minutes.

Serve hot.

Taylor's Tip

For my meat-loving friends, I add cooked, diced sausage to the pasta mixture before baking.

Creamy Mac 'n' Cheese

SERVES 4-6

*It can get pretty cold in Boulder, Colorado, and there is nothing
better to warm us up than our mac 'n' cheese.
Try it paired with our tomato basil soup.*

Ingredients

1 lb elbow pasta

2 large eggs

3 cups of cheddar cheese or combination
of cheddar and jack

1 (12 oz) can of evaporated milk

4 tbsp butter

1 tsp spicy mustard

1/8 tsp pepper

1/8 tsp salt

1/2 tsp red chili pepper flakes

1/4 tsp cayenne pepper

Preparation

Fill a medium pot halfway with water and bring to a boil. Add elbow pasta, return to a boil, and then lower heat to a low boil. Cook according to the instructions on the box.

In large bowl, mix eggs with half the can of evaporated milk, mustard, salt, pepper, and cayenne pepper.

When the pasta is cooked, drain it and return it to the pot. Turn the heat to low and stir in butter until melted.

Add the egg mixture and half of the cheese. Continue to stir over low heat. Gradually stir in remaining evaporated milk and cheese until the mixture is hot and creamy, approximately 5 minutes.

Remove from heat and top with red chili pepper flakes. Serve hot.

Vegetarian Lasagna

SERVES 6-8

My mom sends this dish to me in the mail, but I learned to make it in case I have a craving on a mail holiday or during a blizzard. The vegetables make it lighter than traditional meat lasagna.

Ingredients

1 lb box of lasagna noodles

1 (32 oz) container of ricotta cheese

1 lb mozzarella, shredded

2 (24 oz) jars of marinara sauce

2 cups zucchini and carrots, shredded

Parmesan cheese, grated

Red chili pepper flakes

Preparation

Pre-heat oven to 350 degrees.

Fill a large pot 3/4 of the way full with water and bring to a boil. Add the lasagna noodles and turn heat down to low. Cook pasta according to the directions on the box.

Drain noodles in a colander and carefully separate the noodles with your fingers.

In a medium rectangular 4.8 qt. casserole dish, pour in enough marinara sauce to coat the bottom with a thin layer. Cover with a single layer of noodles. Spread out a thin layer of ricotta cheese over the noodles. Sprinkle 4 tbsp shredded vegetable mixture and sprinkle mozzarella cheese over mixture. Ladle on another thin layer of sauce and add another layer of noodles. Repeat the layers until all the noodles have been used. For the final layer, add just sauce and mozzarella covering the entire dish.

Bake for 50 minutes or until bubbling. Remove from oven and let cool for 10 minutes prior to cutting.

Top with Parmesan cheese and red chili pepper flakes. Serve hot.

> **Note:** *If you would like a meat lasagna, you can substitute our meat sauce (recipe p. 152) for the marinara sauce.*

Risotto

SERVES 2-4

*Is it pasta? Is it rice? Either way, this is great comfort food
that can be served as a side or a main meal.*

Ingredients

1 cup of Arborio rice (Must be Arborio.)

1 (32 oz) box of chicken broth or vegetable broth, or 4 cups of water

2 garlic cloves, minced

4 tbsp olive oil

1/2 cup Parmesan cheese, grated

Pinch of salt and pepper

Red chili pepper flakes

Optional: 1/2 cup frozen peas

Preparation

In a medium pot, warm olive oil over medium-low heat. Add minced garlic and sauté for 2-3 minutes, being careful not to burn the garlic. Add Arborio rice and sauté for approximately 2 more minutes.

Start adding broth 1 cup at a time. Add the salt and pepper after first cup of broth. Then add more liquid once the previous cup of liquid is absorbed. Don't stir. You may only have to use 24 oz (3 cups) of liquid. After approximately 20-25 minutes, all the liquid should be absorbed and the rice should be cooked. The rice should be tender, but not mushy. If it is not tender or all the liquid has not been absorbed, continue to cook until it is. If you are using peas or other frozen vegetable, add to the rice after 10 minutes of cooking time.

Once the rice is cooked, remove from heat, mix with Parmesan cheese, and stir. Serve immediately so the risotto does not get clumpy. Sprinkle with red chili pepper flakes for extra heat.

Penne with Tomatoes, Olives and Artichoke Hearts

SERVES 4-6

Given how simple and easy this is to make, it's surprisingly delicious.
It also features the only kind of hearts we like to eat.

Ingredients

1 lb penne pasta

1 medium onion, diced

3 garlic cloves, minced or pressed

1 (12 oz) jar artichoke hearts

2 (14.5 oz) cans diced tomatoes

1 cup of frozen peas

1/3 cup black olives, chopped

3 tbsp of olive oil

1/8 tsp salt

1/8 tsp pepper

Parmesan cheese, grated

Red chili pepper flakes

Optional: 2 tbsp Greek style yogurt

Preparation

Fill a large pot halfway with water and bring to a boil. Add penne and cook according to the instructions on the box. When cooked, drain in a colander and return to the pot.

Meanwhile, warm olive oil in a large skillet over medium-low heat. Add garlic and onions, and cook until onions are translucent, about 5 minutes.

Add diced tomatoes, olives, artichoke hearts, peas, salt, and pepper, and simmer for approximately 15 minutes. With two minutes left, add the optional Greek style yogurt for a creamier tomato sauce.

Remove from heat and add tomato mixture with the penne in the large pot. Serve hot and topped with grated Parmesan cheese and red chili pepper flakes for extra heat.

Ravioli with Shrimp

SERVES 4

This is a staple of our household because it covers all the food groups and it's hard to mess up!

Ingredients

1 lb bag of frozen ravioli

1 lb bag of frozen shrimp

1 bag of frozen mixed vegetables

1 (24 oz) jar of marinara sauce

2 tbsp olive oil

1/8 tsp salt

1/8 tsp pepper

Parmesan cheese, grated

Preparation

Fill a pot with water. Bring water to a boil.

Meanwhile, put frozen shrimp in a colander under the kitchen faucet and continually run cold water over the shrimp to thaw.

Add ravioli to the boiling water. If the ravioli is vegetarian, cook for 2-4 minutes or until the ravioli floats to the top. If the ravioli is meat-filled, cook for 7-10 minutes or until the pasta is soft.

Warm olive oil in a separate pan on medium-low heat. Add the vegetables and sauté until heated through. Add thawed shrimp to the pan and season with salt and pepper. Cook until shrimp are warm.

When ravioli is done, drain the water and pour the marinara sauce over the ravioli. Add shrimp and vegetable mixture and cook over low heat for a minute, stirring to combine.

Top with Parmesan cheese. Serve hot.

Spicy Shrimp Pasta with Tomatoes and Garlic

SERVES 4

For this pasta, we use our version of an arrabiata sauce, which tastes great with or without the shrimp. We like it really spicy so we even add a half jalapeno with the seeds intact. Any more than half, and you should probably have a fire extinguisher by the table—just in case.

Ingredients

1 lb whole wheat or regular angel hair pasta

3 tbsp olive oil

2 tbsp of chopped fresh basil, dry Italian seasoning, or oregano

1 lb uncooked shrimp, peeled and deveined

1 tbsp red chili pepper flakes

4 garlic cloves, minced

1 tsp cayenne pepper

4 large tomatoes, chopped, or 2 (14.5 oz) cans diced tomatoes

1/8 tsp salt

1/8 tsp pepper

Parmesan cheese, grated

Optional: 1/2 jalapeno chili pepper, chopped with seeds; additional red chili pepper flakes

Preparation

In a medium pot, bring water to a boil and add pasta. Cook according to directions. When finished, drain in a colander.

In a large, deep skillet, warm olive oil over medium-low heat. Add garlic and sauté, being careful not to burn the garlic. Add the shrimp and sauté until pink. Remove the shrimp from the pan and set aside. Add diced tomatoes, red chili pepper flakes, chopped basil, cayenne pepper, salt, and pepper, and sauté for approximately 5 minutes. Return shrimp to the pan and cook for 1 additional minute, stirring to blend the flavors.

Mound a portion of pasta on each plate, and spoon shrimp mixture onto the pasta. Grate Parmesan cheese over the top, and sprinkle on additional red chili pepper flakes if desired.

Serve hot.

Taylor's Tip

If you don't have fresh shrimp on hand, you can use frozen, cooked shrimp instead, and it will still taste great. To thaw the shrimp, place them in a colander and let cold water run over them for at least 3-5 minutes. Then add the thawed pre-cooked shrimp to your skillet in the last couple of minutes to heat through.

Penne with Tuna, Tomatoes, Garlic, and Capers

SERVES 4

This is like a puttanesca sauce, but with tuna instead of anchovies.
It's rich with a great kick—kinda like Jackie Chan.

Ingredients

1 lb box of whole wheat or regular penne

3 tbsp olive oil

4 garlic cloves, minced

1 tbsp capers, chopped

1/4 cup black olives, chopped

1/4 cup jalapenos, diced

1 tsp red chili pepper flakes

2 (14.5 oz) cans of crushed tomatoes

1 (5 oz) can of albacore tuna, drained

1 cup fresh basil leaves, gently shredded

1/8 tsp salt

1/8 tsp pepper

Parmesan cheese, grated

Preparation

Fill pot with water and bring to a boil. Add the penne when you are ready to begin cooking the sauce. Cook pasta according to the instructions on the box. When the pasta is cooked, drain it and return it to the pot.

In a large skillet, warm the olive oil on medium-low heat. Add the garlic and cook for approximately 5 minutes, being careful not to burn it.

Add capers, olives, jalapenos, red chili pepper flakes, tomatoes, basil, salt, and pepper. Simmer for approximately 8 minutes. Add the tuna and continue cooking about another 5-7 minutes until the sauce has reduced.

Pour sauce into the pot with the penne and stir to combine.

Serve hot, topped with grated Parmesan cheese.

DINNER ENTREES

1. Delicious from A to T

2. Hamburgers or Turkey Burgers

3. Black Bean Veggie Burgers

4. Tilapia Grill

5. Ahi Sliders

6. Roasted Chicken

7. Chicken Curry

8. Chicken Parmesan

9. Turkey Vegetable Medley

10. Meatballs

11. Asian Stir-Fry Bowl

12. Lazu Pork Ribs

13. Korean Pork Tenderloin Roast

14. Southwestern Steak Tacos

15. Lamb Chops with Garlic

16. Egg Drop Ramen

Matching our variety of college buddies, we have included a cornucopia of dinner items. We offer recipes for not only our mainstay, chicken, but also beef, pork, lamb, turkey, fish, bean, and eggs. You could start at the top of the alphabet with the Ahi Sliders and end up with our turkey recipe (Turkey Vegetable Medley). They are all delicious.

Hamburgers or Turkey Burgers

SERVES 6-8

What's more American than a basic burger? Maybe a basic burger wrapped in the American flag. But that would be hard to digest.

Ingredients

2 lbs frozen burger patties or fresh ground beef or turkey meat

1/2 head lettuce

2 tomatoes

1 large onion

Pickles

Hamburger buns

1/2 tsp salt

1/2 tsp pepper

Olive oil spray (We like PAM's.)

Condiments (mayonnaise, mustard, ranch dressing, hot sauce)

Optional: Cheese

Preparation

Plug in your electric grill to allow it to heat up. It's ready for cooking when the red light turns off.

While your electric grill is heating up, prepare your other ingredients. Wash all the vegetables, slice the tomato, and tear the lettuce leaves and pat them dry. If you are using fresh meat, add a pinch of salt and pepper to the meat, and then use your hands to shape it into patties approximately 1/2 inch thick and the size of a hamburger bun.

When the electric grill is ready, add olive oil spray to the surface. Place patties on the grill. After a few minutes, flip the patties onto the other side. The longer you cook them, the more well done they will be. Beef burgers can be eaten when they are pink at the center, but turkey burgers should be well done all the way through. If you like your burger buns toasted, put them in the toaster now.

Once the burgers are cooked to your liking, remove them from the grill and let them rest on a plate. If you are using cheese, open the lid of the grill and place the cheese on the patties to melt before you take the patties off the grill.

Once the patties are finished, place a patty on each bun and add condiments and toppings to your liking—including tomato, onion, lettuce, mustard, etc.

Taylor's Tip
. . . .
Hamburgers can be turned into sliders (mini-hamburgers) by buying slider-sized buns and forming smaller patties the size of flattened ping pong balls to fit those buns. Sliders are a great party food or half-time snack during a football game.

Black Bean Veggie Burgers

SERVES 4

*Sometimes we're in the mood for a vegetarian meal, but we still want
something hearty to sink our teeth into. These burgers are a great option.
They take a little more effort than meat burgers, but they are
equally tasty and healthier than their meat-based brethren.*

Ingredients

1 (14.5 oz) can of black beans, rinsed

1 large carrot, diced

1/2 cup frozen peas, thawed

1/2 onion, diced

3 cloves garlic, minced

1 egg

1/2 cup panko (Japanese bread crumbs), or
regular bread crumbs

1 tbsp chili powder

1 tsp cumin

1 tsp red chili pepper flakes

1 tbsp olive oil, plus oil for baking sheet

1/4 tsp salt

Optional: 1/2 cup walnuts, chopped

Preparation

Pre-heat oven to 350 degrees. Lightly coat baking sheet with olive oil.

In a mixing bowl, add beans and lightly mash. Mix in carrot, peas, garlic, walnuts
(optional), and olive oil.

In a separate bowl, add egg, salt, chili powder, cumin, and red chili pepper flakes
and stir. Add egg mixture and panko to the bean mixture and mix together. Once evenly
combined, form four patties approximately 1/2 inch thick and the size of hamburger bun
and place on the baking sheet.

Bake for approximately 20-24 minutes, flipping the patties halfway through.

Serve hot, with or without a bun and your favorite condiments.

Tilapia Grill

SERVES 2

When we're feeling like lighter fare, tilapia is our go-to fish. It's inexpensive to buy, simple to cook, and makes for a healthy entrée. That is especially important if we are each having a gallon of ice cream for dessert.

Ingredients

1 lb of tilapia fillet or other thin cut fish like sole or red snapper

3 tbsp of fresh lemon juice

2 tbsp of chopped parsley

2 cloves of garlic, minced

1 tbsp olive oil

1/8 tsp salt

Optional: 1/4 cup crushed pistachios

Preparation

Pre-heat electric grill to medium high heat.

Mix lemon juice, parsley, olive oil, salt, and garlic in a shallow bowl and dip fish into the mixture.

Grill for approximately for 6 minutes on each side until fish is white and opaque all the way through. If fully cooked, fish flakes when it's cut. Top with crushed pistachios for added flavor.

Serve hot.

Ahi Sliders

SERVES 2

For us California guys, we love our ahi best in sushi.
But the next best place is in a slider, especially if that slider is
served with a side of ahi tuna maki.

Ingredients

1 lb of yellowfin tuna, cut in 1/4 lb pieces

1-½ tsp soy sauce

3 tbsp mayonnaise

Slider buns (mini hamburger buns)

2 cups mixed greens

Aioli spread (recipe p. 148)

Olive oil spray (We like PAM's.)

Optional: 1/2 tsp wasabi paste

Preparation

Prepare electric grill for cooking by coating it with olive oil spray.

Mix soy sauce and mayonnaise in a bowl. Add wasabi paste if you like some heat. Coat tuna in mixture until evenly covered.

Place fish on the grill and cook on each side for 1-2 minutes, depending on how cooked you like your fish.

Place on a bun and top with mixed greens and aioli. Serve hot.

Taylor's Tip

· · · · · · · · · · · · · ·

In case you were
wondering where the
ahi is in this recipe,
yellowtail tuna is a
type of ahi.

Egg and Cheese Bagel, recipe page 42

Smoothies, recipes page 49

Blueberry and Banana Pancakes, recipe page 45

Loco Moco, recipe page 43

Breakfast Burrito, recipe page 41

Faux French Croissants with Ricotta Cheese and Chocolate Chips, recipe page 44

Grilled Cheese, recipe page 56

Turkey and Pepper Jack Cheese Wrap, recipe page 58

Croque Monsieur and Croque Madame, recipe page 60

Cuban Style Sandwich, recipe page 62

Creamy Tomato Basil Soup, recipe page 75

Vegetable Barley Soup, recipe page 74

Bow Tie Pasta with Pesto/Pine Nuts, recipe page 82

Ravioli with Shrimp, recipe page 88

Creamy Mac 'n' Cheese, recipe page 84

Vegetarian Lasagna, recipe page 85

Spicy Shrimp Pasta, recipe page 89

Penne with Tomatoes, Olives and Artichoke Hearts, recipe page 87

Ahi Sliders, recipe page 96

Meatballs, recipe page 101

Southwestern Steak Tacos, recipe page 105

Egg Drop Ramen, recipe page 107

Asian Stir-Fry Bowl, recipe page 102

Roasted Chicken, recipe page 97

Lamb Chops with Garlic, recipe page 106

Chopped Chicken Salad, recipe page 111

Chicken Lettuce Wraps, recipe page 116

Tomato and Mozzarella Salad, recipe page 71

Potato Salad with Mustard/Horseradish, recipe page 126

Moroccan Couscous with Dried Fruit, recipe page 121

Oven Roasted Vegetables, recipe page 125

Apple Betty, recipe page 138

Roasted Chicken

SERVES 6

We included a special section in our cookbook that explains ten ways to use a pre-roasted chicken that you buy from the store. However, when we want to have a special dinner to impress the girls next door, we make our own roasted chicken and light the one candle we keep for this exact purpose (impressing them). Of course, you could also roast your own whole chicken to use in some of the ten ways.

Ingredients

4-5 lb roasting chicken

2 tbsp olive oil

1 lemon, cut into slices

Pinch of salt and pepper

Preparation

Pre-heat oven to 350 degrees. Prepare chicken by taking out the neck and kidney from the cavity. This may seem gross at first, but just do it. It will be over quickly.

To keep the meat moist, position the chicken breast down in a roasting pan with or without a rack. A rack allows the fat to drip in the pan, but it's not necessary.

Rub olive oil over the entire chicken, sprinkle with salt and pepper, and stuff lemon slices in the cavity. Cook for approximately 1 hour and 45 minutes or until the leg pulls off easily and the meat is no longer pink. White meat always cooks faster, so check the dark meat to make sure the chicken is done.

Remove from the oven and allow to rest for 10-15 minutes to keep the juices from escaping, which would result in dry meat. Carve and serve immediately.

Chicken Curry

SERVES 4

This Indian-style dish is an easy way to spice up a chicken dinner.
When we can't afford a plane ticket, whipping up international fare
is the next best option.

Ingredients

1-1/2 lbs boneless, skinless chicken thighs cut into 2 inch pieces

2-3 tbsp olive oil

2 (14.5 oz) cans crushed tomatoes

1 large onion, diced

3 garlic cloves, chopped

1 tbsp Tandoori paste (We prefer Patak's.)

1 cup of Greek style yogurt

1 cup frozen green peas

1/4 tsp salt

Rice for serving

Preparation

Warm the olive oil on low to medium heat in a pot and add the onion and garlic. Sauté for 5 minutes, or until the onions are translucent. Increase the heat to medium, and cook the chicken for 3 minutes on each side until nicely browned.

Add crushed tomatoes, salt and Tandoori paste, and bring to a boil. Reduce heat to low and simmer covered for 1 hour.

In the last 15 minutes, add the 1/2 cup green peas and the yogurt.

Serve hot over any type of rice, preferably jasmine rice.

Chicken Parmesan

SERVES 4

*Like a true master of disguise, chicken takes on many forms in this book.
Here it's going Italian style for a quick and easy dish that tastes like restaurant
food and looks like you skipped class to have time to make it.*

Ingredients

4 boneless, skinless chicken breasts

1 cup Parmesan cheese, grated

1 (24 oz) jar of marinara sauce

4 slices of mozzarella cheese

1 cup panko or bread crumbs

1/2 cup flour

2 eggs

1/4 tsp salt

Preparation

Pre-heat the oven to 350 degrees.

Coat the bottom of an 8x8 or 2 qt. glass cooking dish (such as Pyrex) with a thin layer of red sauce.

To prepare for breading the chicken, set three shallow bowls on the counter. Fill one with the flour and salt. Crack the eggs into the second bowl and whisk them. Fill the third bowl with the panko or bread crumbs. Then dip the chicken into the flour to lightly coat it, dip it next into the egg, and last dip it into the panko or bread crumbs.

Set each breaded chicken breast on red sauce in the glass dish and sprinkle the chicken breasts with approximately 1 tbsp of Parmesan cheese each. Pour the remaining marinara sauce over the chicken breasts, and then sprinkle on the rest of the Parmesan cheese.

Bake for approximately 45 minutes, placing a slice of mozzarella cheese on top of each breast for the last 5 minutes.

Serve hot with your favorite pasta.

Turkey Vegetable Medley

SERVES 4

This harmonious blend of meat and veggies hits the spot at any time of the day. On the weekends, we like to add scrambled eggs to it and eat it for a second breakfast.

Ingredients

1 lb of ground turkey

1 red onion, diced

1 large carrot, chopped into 1 inch pieces

1 green bell pepper, chopped into 1 inch pieces

1 (14.5 oz) can of black beans

2 tbsp chopped cilantro

1 cup frozen corn

5 tbsp of olive oil

2 tbsp of your favorite hot sauce

1 tsp of cumin

1/2 tsp of pepper

1/2 tsp of salt

1/2 tsp of garlic powder

Optional: flour tortillas

Preparation

Heat 2 tbsp olive oil in a medium skillet. Add ground turkey, salt, pepper, cumin, and garlic powder. Simmer on low-medium heat, stirring often for approximately 8-10 minutes until the meat is no longer pink inside. Remove pan from heat and transfer turkey to a plate.

In the same (now empty) skillet, heat the remaining 3 tbsp of olive oil. Add bell pepper, red onion, and carrot, and sauté for 4 minutes. Add black beans, cilantro, corn, and hot sauce. Stir for 1 minute to combine and then add the cooked turkey back to the skillet. Cook for 1 more minute until all the flavors have combined and everything is hot.

Serve hot with a flour tortilla or on its own as a low-carb option.

Meatballs

*Meatballs are another staple in our household. We eat them separately,
add them to our favorite pasta dish, or juggle them to impress houseguests.*

Ingredients

1 egg

1/4 cup panko (Japanese bread crumbs)

1 lb ground turkey or 1/2 lb ground turkey mixed with 1/2 lb ground pork

1 tsp cumin

1 tsp chili powder

1 tsp red chili pepper flakes

1 tbsp chopped cilantro or parsley

1 tsp olive oil

1/4 tsp salt

Pinch of pepper

Olive oil spray for baking sheet (We like PAM's.)

Preparation

Pre-heat oven to 350 degrees. Coat a baking sheet with olive oil spray.

In a mixing bowl, combine meat and the remaining ingredients. Mix with your hands and then form into balls the size of ping-pong balls, placing them on the oiled baking sheet as you go.

Place the baking sheet in the oven and cook the meatballs for 7 minutes on each side.

Check one meatball to see if it's cooked through. When it is no longer pink in the middle, take the meatballs out of the oven and garnish with marinara sauce or add to your favorite pasta.

Serve hot.

Taylor's Tip

. . . .

*Sometimes we end
up with leftover
meatballs, which are
great for making into
a meatball sandwich.
Simply add them to
a bun or baguette
and top with
marinara sauce and
Parmesan cheese.*

Asian Stir-Fry Bowl

SERVES 2-4

If you are looking for a good recipe for leftovers, this it is. It's easy to make a lot of it, it's filling, and somehow we never get tired of eating it!

Ingredients

2 cups white rice (or brown rice as a healthier alternative)

2 cups of water

1 bag frozen Asian vegetable medley or other chopped frozen vegetables

1 lb beef, chicken, or tofu diced into bite-sized pieces

2 tbsp soy sauce

2 tsp garlic powder

2 tbsp water

2 tbsp vegetable oil

Preparation

Rinse 2 cups of rice in a strainer until the water runs clean. Add rinsed rice and 2 cups of room temperature water to the rice cooker and cover.

Steam or microwave frozen vegetables according to the package to remove excess water.

Pre-heat a large pan on high heat and add vegetable oil. Once the oil is popping, add meat or tofu along with a mixture of the soy sauce and garlic powder. Stir-fry until the meat is cooked almost all the way through or the tofu is nicely browned. Add pre-steamed vegetables to the pan, and water if necessary. Continue cooking over low heat until vegetables are warm but not soggy.

Spread rice on the bottom of your plate, and then top with stir-fry mixture. Serve hot.

Note: *If we are using a **rice cooker,** we use a 2 cups water to 2 cups rice ratio. If we are cooking **stove top,** we use a 2 cups water to 1 cup of rice ratio.*

Taylor's Tip

* * * * * * * * * * * * * * * *

Frozen vegetables are good for a quick meal that requires less prep. However, when we are feeling more motivated, we substitute fresh vegetables such as peppers, broccoli, and snap peas. If you are using fresh vegetables, simply chop them into bite-sized pieces and steam them for about 10 minutes before adding them to the stir-fry.

Lazu Pork Ribs

SERVES 6 - 8

For carnivores, these pork ribs really hit the spot (especially when done on the grill). But be warned, this is probably not the best meal for a date or when you are wearing a white tux. Below is the easy oven version of the recipe.

Ribs
Ingredients

3-4 lbs of pork ribs

1/2 cup sugar

1/2 tsp salt

Preparation

Sprinkle sugar and salt over pork ribs. Marinate in the refrigerator overnight or at least 6 hours prior to cooking.

Sauce
Ingredients

1/4 tsp ground ginger

1 cup ketchup

1 tbsp hoisin sauce

1 garlic clove, minced

1/3 cup brown sugar

1 tbsp honey

1 tbsp soy sauce

Preparation

Bake pre-marinated pork ribs for 1 hour at 350 degrees meat-side up (without the sauce).

While ribs are baking, mix the sauce ingredients together.

After the initial hour of baking, turn ribs over, brush on enough sauce to cover ribs, and bake for another 15 minutes.

Turn ribs over, brush on the rest of the sauce, and bake for another 15 minutes.

Serve hot with your favorite side dish.

Korean Pork Tenderloin Roast

SERVES 4-6

We love chicken, but sometimes we get a taste for something a little different. Pork is a great, lean alternative that's easy to prepare and sure to impress a date or your parents when they fly in for your Ultimate Frisbee championships.

Ingredients

1-1/2 lbs of boneless pork tenderloin roast

2 tbsp of soy sauce

1 tsp of sesame oil

2 tbsp of brown sugar

1 tbsp of apple cider vinegar or white wine vinegar

2 tsp of garlic, minced

1 tsp hot mustard

1 tsp red chili pepper flakes

Preparation

To prepare the pork for cooking, cut out the white membrane covering the loin with a sharp, thin-bladed knife if this has not been done already before packaging.

Mix soy sauce, sesame oil, garlic, sugar, mustard, chili pepper flakes, and vinegar in a large plastic bag, and then place pork loin in the bag.

Marinate overnight or at least 2-3 hours.

Cook the marinated loin in an oven pre-heated to 350 degrees for 45 minutes or until the pork is medium-well done.

Serve hot.

Taylor's Tip

. . . .

Any leftovers can be used to make our Cuban Style sandwich into a true Cubano with a slight Asian twist. (See p. 62, Sandwiches chapter, for recipe.)

Southwestern Steak Tacos

SERVES 4

We may live in Colorado, but we can't get away from our Southern California roots and that area's love for tacos.

Ingredients

Corn tortillas

1 lb of skirt steak

1 cup frozen corn

1 red bell pepper, seeded and thinly sliced

1/2 lb cheddar or jack cheese, grated

2 small tomatoes, chopped

2 tbsp olive oil

Juice of one lime

1 tsp cumin

1/2 tsp pepper

1/4 tsp salt

1 scallion, chopped (use white bulb part, or green part as well)

Sour cream

Salsa (recipe p. 147)

Optional: 4 more scallions, chopped; 2 tablespoons cilantro, chopped

Preparation

Pre-heat your oven to 250 degrees. Place tortillas on a baking sheet and warm in the oven until you are ready to make your tacos.

Warm the olive oil in a medium pan or skillet over low-medium heat until hot. Mix cumin, black pepper, and lime juice with corn, red bell pepper, and 1 scallion. Sauté the mixture for 5 minutes and then remove the pan from the heat. Cover with foil to keep the vegetables warm.

Taylor's Tip
. . . .
This is a great meal to make with friends. Everyone can join in and build their own tacos together.

Season steak with salt. Grill steak for 5-6 minutes on your electric grill until it's only slightly pink in the center (or just re-heat it in the micro-wave if you are using leftovers).

Once steak is finished, let it cool slightly and then slice it into strips on a cutting board. Build your tacos by first adding steak to a warm tortilla and then spooning vegetables over the steak. Top with sour cream, grated cheese, tomatoes, cilantro, scallions, and your favorite salsa.

Serve hot.

Lamb Chops with Garlic

SERVES 2

When our bank account is full because our parents or the Tooth Fairy stopped by,
we sometimes splurge to make one of our favorite meals. It's one of
the few things that we actually broil, because it tastes so good that way.
However, you can grill them as well.

Ingredients

1 lb lamb rib chops, around 3-4

1 tbsp olive oil

2 garlic cloves, minced

Preparation

Put olive oil, garlic, and chops in a large plastic bag. Shake to cover the chops evenly. Let marinate for at least 20 minutes. Pre-heat broiler to 475-500 degrees. When ready, position 3-4 chops on the broiler pan. Cook on one side for approximately 2-3 minutes and flip and cook for additional 2-3 minutes. We prefer medium rare chops that are on the pink side, but you can cook them longer for well-done chops.

Serve hot.

Egg Drop Ramen

SERVES 1

Even James Bond always had a Plan B. This is our go-to meal when all else fails or we are being chased by a super villain and need to make dinner in a hurry.

Ingredients

1 ramen noodle packet

1 egg

Pinch of salt and pepper

Hot sauce

Optional: second egg, sunny side up

Preparation

In a small pot, bring 2 cups of water to a boil. Add a pinch of salt and pepper prior to boiling.

Add the ramen noodles and cook for approximately 2 minutes. Gently crack an egg and drop it into the center of noodles.

Cook for 2 more minutes.

Drain in colander. Be careful not to crack the yolk. Serve hot in a bowl topped with a few squirts of your favorite hot sauce. For extra egginess, you can also top it with a sunny side up egg!

ROASTED CHICKEN:
10 DIFFERENT MEALS

17

1. The Many Possibilities of Pre-Roasted Chicken

2. Tortilla Soup

3. Chopped Chicken Salad

4. Chicken Quesadilla

5. Chicken Enchiladas

6. Chicken Burrito

7. Chicken Fajitas

8. Chicken Lettuce Wraps

9. Nachos in a Bag

10. Grilled Chicken Panini

11. Chicken Pita

THE MANY POSSIBILITIES OF
PRE-ROASTED CHICKEN

A pre-roasted chicken is one of the best budget food items—whether you buy it cooked at the store or roast a whole chicken yourself to have on hand. It's easy to use and the possibilities are unlimited, but we have ten of our favorite ways for you here. One whole chicken goes a long way. So you can either make the full servings of one of these recipes to serve a group, or use part of the chicken and try a couple recipes throughout the week. The number of servings for each recipe depends on the quantity of your leftovers.

HOW TO CARVE CHICKEN

(If you have roasted the chicken yourself, let it sit for approximately 5-10 minutes prior to carving.) Begin carving by gently bending the legs away from the body. You may not even need a knife to remove the legs. Next, use a chef's knife to cut a leg and thigh apart at the joint. Next, cut along the breast bone with the same knife, separating the breast into two sides. You can either leave the entire breast intact after removing it, or finish cutting each breast on a cutting board. You may also carve pieces of the breast while it is still attached to the chicken. Last but not least, remove the wings using a chef's knife to cut the wings at the joint away from the body of the chicken.

Tortilla Soup

SERVES 6-8

This is a perfect combination of all of our favorite ingredients.

Ingredients

1 3-lb pre-roasted chicken or about 5 cups of shredded chicken

1 onion, diced

2 (14.5 oz) cans of diced tomatoes

1 (32 oz) box of chicken broth

1 (32 oz) box of beef broth

1/2 (32 oz) box of chicken or beef broth

4 small (5.5 oz) cans spicy tomato juice (V8 is our favorite.)

Cheddar cheese, grated

2 avocados, sliced

4 tbsp olive oil

1 tbsp chili powder

1 tbsp cumin

1 tsp Worcestershire sauce

1 tsp pepper

1/2 tsp salt

Bag of tortilla chips

Optional: 1 jalapeno chili pepper, diced or 1/2 tsp cayenne pepper

Preparation

Warm olive oil in a large pot over medium-low heat. Add onion to the pot and sauté until translucent.

Add 2-1/2 boxes of broth, chili powder, cumin, V8 juice, Worcestershire sauce, salt, and pepper. Bring to boil. Add shredded chicken and diced tomatoes. Turn heat down and simmer for 1 hour to let the flavors blend. If the soup is too thick, add more broth and tomato juice to your preferred thickness. Ladle into bowls and top with broken up tortilla chips, sliced avocado, and grated cheese.

Serve hot.

Taylor's Tip
. . . .
When I'm in the mood for a spicier soup, I add a diced whole jalapeno chili.

Chopped Chicken Salad

SERVES 2

*For those of you who think salad is too light to be filling, this recipe
may change your mind. It's jam packed with meat, cheese, beans, and veggies
to offer a well-rounded and very filling meal.*

Ingredients

1/2 head of romaine lettuce or
green leaf lettuce

1 cup chicken, shredded

1 (15 oz) can garbanzo beans, drained
and rinsed

1 tomato, chopped

1 avocado, cubed

2 carrots, chopped

1 cup frozen corn, thawed in the microwave

8 oz of jack cheese, cubed

2 eggs, hard-boiled and sliced

Cooked bacon or salami, chopped

Vinaigrette (recipe p. 142)

Preparation

Chop lettuce into bite-sized pieces and place in a colander or salad spinner and rinse.
Pat lettuce dry with a paper towel to remove water. In a large bowl, add the lettuce and the
rest of ingredients and toss with a vinaigrette or Italian dressing.

Chicken Quesadilla

SERVES 1

Who knew flat food could taste so good?

Ingredients

1 cup chicken, shredded

1 cup cheddar cheese, grated

1 flour tortilla

1 tsp canola oil

Optional: sliced avocados, chopped onions, sliced scallions, and your favorite hot sauce

Preparation

Coat a small skillet with canola oil. Warm at low-medium heat. Add flour tortilla and line one side with chicken pieces and cheese.

Fold tortilla in half and let heat on low for approximately 1-2 minutes. Turn over and continue heating on low for another minute. Once cheese is melted, take off heat and set aside.

Cut in thirds and serve hot topped with sliced avocados, your favorite hot sauce, etc.

Chicken Enchiladas

SERVES 6 (MAKES 12 ENCHILADAS)

Although these look like little edible sleeping bags of tastiness,
we wouldn't recommend trying to make them while camping.
It's a hassle to pack the oven in the car.

Ingredients

2 cups chicken, shredded

12 corn tortillas

2 cups shredded cheddar and jack cheese, mixed

1 (28 oz) can of enchilada sauce

1 tbsp black olives, chopped

3 tbsp of green chilies or jalapenos, diced

1 tsp cumin

Optional: olives, sliced avocados, diced scallions, or sour cream for garnish

Preparation

Pre-heat oven to 350 degrees.

Heat a non-oiled skillet. Warm tortillas one at a time and set them aside.

In a mixing bowl, combine chicken pieces, 1-1/2 cups cheese, green chilies, cumin, olives, and 1 cup of enchilada sauce. Reserve 1/2 cup of cheese to top the enchiladas.

Line the bottom of a 4.8 qt. glass baking dish with 1 ladle of enchilada sauce. Assemble enchiladas on a cutting board by placing approximately 3 tbsp worth of the chicken mixture in each tortilla and rolling them into cylinders. Place each enchilada in the dish with the seam facing down.

Once all enchiladas are in the dish, pour the remaining enchilada sauce over all the enchiladas, and sprinkle with remaining cheese.

Bake at 350 degrees for approximately 30 minutes until bubbling. Remove from the oven and top with any optional garnishes.

Serve hot.

Chicken Burrito

SERVES 4

Who doesn't love a burrito? If you know someone, have them call us and we'll make this one for them to change their mind. (Just kidding!)

Ingredients

2 cups chicken, shredded

1 cup of white rice

1 (16 oz) can refried beans

2 cups water or chicken broth

2 cups cheddar cheese, shredded

2 tomatoes, chopped

1 cup frozen corn

Salsa (recipe p. 147)

4 large flour tortillas

Optional: sliced avocados, diced scallions, or sour cream for garnish

Preparation

In a small pot, add rice and two cups of water or broth and bring to a boil. Reduce heat and cover, simmering for approximately 20 minutes. Place frozen corn in microwave safe container with 1/2 cup water and cook on high for 2 minutes.

Once rice is cooked, place tortillas on a plate and add a quarter of each of the beans, rice, cheese, corn, and tomato. Fold one side, both ends, and then other side to form burrito.

Place burrito in a microwave safe bowl with the seam down and cover. Cook on high for 3 minutes. Using a knife, make slices into the top of the burrito and cook on high for another 2 minutes, or until the beans are hot all the way through.

Top with a scoop of your favorite salsa and any optional garnishes. Serve hot.

Chicken Fajitas

SERVES 2-4

Serve these sizzling hot or adopt a pet dragon to blow fire
on them right before you dig in.

Ingredients

3 cups of chicken, shredded

1 onion, cut into strips

5 tbsp olive oil

1/2 cup water

1 bag frozen red and green peppers or 1 red
and 1 green pepper, chopped lengthwise in
2 inch pieces

1 packet fajita seasoning or your own fajita
mix (See recipe below.)

Flour tortillas

3 avocados

Salsa (recipe p. 147)

Preparation

In a bowl, add fajita seasoning packet, with 2 tbsp olive oil, and shredded chicken. Coat chicken evenly. You can add less seasoning for a less salty taste or use our fajita mix recipe, which is a tasty, low-salt alternative.

In a medium skillet or pan on low to medium heat, add remaining olive oil and onion, and sauté for 5 minutes or until onions are clear. Add chicken, vegetables, and 1/2 cup water, and continue cooking for 3-5 minutes or until vegetables are soft.

Warm flour tortillas in a non-oiled skillet or pan for 1-2 minutes. Put aside.

Scoop chicken and vegetable mixture into tortilla and add sliced avocado and favorite salsa.

Serve hot.

Fajita Seasoning Recipe

3 tbsp olive oil

3 tbsp water

1 tbsp chili powder

1-1/2 tsp paprika

1 tsp garlic powder

1 tsp oregano

1 tsp black pepper

Pinch of salt

2 tbsp fresh lime juice

Mix into a paste. Add more water to dilute.

Chicken Lettuce Wraps

SERVES 2

These make a great light meal or an appetizer for an Asian-inspired dinner party.
Plus, we always have fun eating food wrapped in lettuce.

Ingredients

1 cup of chicken, shredded

4 butter lettuce leaves, separated, washed, and patted dry

1 cup of peanuts, chopped

1 bunch of scallions, chopped or small onion, diced

2-3 tbsp Asian Vinaigrette (recipe p. 143)

1/2 tsp hoisin sauce

Optional: Hot sauce or powdered ginger

Preparation

In a mixing bowl, combine shredded chicken, peanuts, scallions, hoisin sauce, and 2-3 tbsp Asian Vinaigrette dressing.

Scoop approximately 2 tbsp of mixture onto each piece of lettuce.

Top with hot sauce (our favorite is Sriracha) for extra punch or powdered ginger for extra flavor.

Nachos in a Bag

SERVES 4

This on-the-go meal takes vending machine chips to a whole new level.

Ingredients

1 cup chicken, shredded

4 small to medium individual bags of corn or tortilla chips

1 (16 oz) can of refried beans

1 tsp olive oil

2 cups of cheddar cheese, grated

1 (16 oz) container of sour cream

Hot sauce

Preparation

Take individual bags of corn or tortilla chips and cut each bag in half. In the meantime, heat the refried beans in a small pot with olive oil over low heat. Once the beans are heated, remove from heat. Scoop desired amount of shredded chicken, beans, cheese, and sour cream into bag and mix with a fork. Top with your favorite hot sauce.

Serve warm.

Grilled Chicken Panini

SERVES 1

Electric grills turn everyday sandwiches into melted delicacies.

Ingredients

1 cup chicken, shredded

2 Provolone cheese slices

1 tomato, sliced

Bread of choice

Olive oil spray (We like PAM's.)

Optional: peperoncini, other condiments

Preparation

Pre-heat electric grill and coat with olive oil spray. Assemble sandwich by layering cheese, chicken, and tomato on bread of choice. Place on the grill and cook on each side for approximately 3 minutes. Remove and serve hot.

Chicken Pita

SERVES 1

Pita pockets make for a much tastier and less messy meal than filling shirt pockets with sandwich fixings.

Ingredients

1 cup chicken, shredded

1 pita bread pocket

2 slices of Provolone or jack cheese

1 tomato, sliced

Mixed greens

Optional: mustard, mayonnaise

Preparation

Spread condiments on the inside of the pita bread. Stuff with chicken, lettuce, tomato, and cheese.

SIDE DISHES AND VEGETABLES

18

1. Recipes Both You & Mom Will Love

2. Moroccan Couscous with Dried Fruit

3. Steamed Green Beans with Olive Oil and Lemon

4. Yams with Orange Juice and Cumin

5. Broccoli with Orange Juice and Soy Sauce

6. Oven Roasted Vegetables

7. Potato Salad with Mustard and Horseradish

8. Quinoa with Zucchini

9. Potatoes – Baked/Boiled Red or White/Mashed/
   (also Easy Gravy)

10. Corn on the Cob

This chapter has everything from a super grain (quinoa), to broccoli, to green beans, to yams, to something that sounds like a bird call (couscous), so your mother will be happy that she bought this book for you. No longer will she complain that you are not eating your vegetables or grains. For those of you who stick to the basics like potatoes and corn, we have recipes for you too.

Moroccan Couscous with Dried Fruit

SERVES 4

Couscous is a great option when we are in need of a change from our old stand-by, rice. It also sounds fancy when we serve it to guests.

Ingredients

2 cups of chicken broth, vegetable broth, or water

1 box of couscous

1/2 cup raisins and/or chopped dried apricots

Optional: red, yellow, or green bell peppers, diced

Preparation

In a medium pot, add couscous, broth or water, and any optional vegetables. Bring to a boil. Turn off heat, transfer to another burner, and let sit for 5 minutes. In the last 2 minutes, add the raisins or the apricots.

Serve hot.

Steamed Green Beans with Olive Oil and Lemon

SERVES 4

Green beans always seemed a little dry and flavorless to me. But now due to my new love of olive oil, I just need a little drizzle and I can eat my beans!

Ingredients

1 lb green beans, washed and ends clipped

1 tbsp fresh lemon juice

1 tbsp olive oil

Preparation

Fill a medium pot with about 1 inch of water, and place a vegetable steamer in the pot. The water should just touch the bottom of the steamer. Place green beans in the steamer, and cook on high for approximately 10 minutes with the pot covered. The green beans will be cooked if they are soft when pierced with a fork.

Once cooked, put the green beans in a shallow bowl, and toss them with lemon juice and olive oil.

Serve hot or cold.

Yams with Orange Juice and Cumin

SERVES 2

*The nutty, peppery flavor of the cumin compliments the sweet yams
and orange juice really well. Experimenting is the key to our cooking.
This is the stuff gourmet cooking is made of!*

Ingredients

1/2 lb yams, peeled and sliced in
1 inch rounds

3 large oranges, squeezed for the juice, or
1-1/2 cups orange juice

1 tbsp cumin

1 tbsp butter

Preparation

Pre-heat oven to 350 degrees.

Place butter in a microwave safe bowl, cover, and heat in microwave on low for 15-20 seconds, or until melted.

In a small bowl, mix the melted butter, cumin, and orange juice. Scoop out 1/2 cup of liquid and reserve for later. Add yams to the bowl and toss to evenly cover them.

Transfer the yams to a glass baking dish. Bake for approximately 40 minutes, occasionally flipping the yams and drizzling them with the reserved juice mixture. Yams are finished when you can easily pierce them with a fork.

Serve hot.

Broccoli with Orange Juice and Soy Sauce

SERVES 2-4

Instead of steaming with water, we add extra flavor to the broccoli by steaming it with orange juice and soy sauce. You'll never look at broccoli the same way again.

Ingredients

1 lb of broccoli, cut into florets

2/3 cup orange juice

1 tbsp soy sauce

1/4 cup water

Preparation

In a medium pot, add orange juice, water, and soy sauce, and place steamer in the pot. Place the broccoli florets in the steamer, cover the pot, and cook on high for approximately 10 minutes.

Transfer broccoli to a shallow serving bowl, and drizzle any remaining liquid from the pot over the broccoli.

Serve hot.

Oven Roasted Vegetables

SERVES 6

*These are great on their own as a vegetarian meal or as a
side dish with our roasted chicken.*

Ingredients

1 large red onion, cut in quarters

2 large carrots, peeled and cut in 3 inch pieces

2 large yams, unpeeled and cut in 3 inch
pieces

4 medium red potatoes, unpeeled and cut in
quarters

6 garlic cloves, minced

2 tbsp olive oil

1 tbsp soy sauce

1 tbsp honey

1/8 tsp salt

1/8 tsp pepper

Preparation

Pre-heat the oven to 425 degrees. In a mixing bowl, combine all the ingredients and toss.

Transfer vegetables to baking sheet or large glass baking dish, and bake for approximately
45 minutes (or until the veggies are easily pierced with a fork).

Serve hot.

Potato Salad with Mustard and Horseradish

SERVES 4

*Our version of potato salad is much lighter than traditional potato salad,
which makes it a great side for heartier dishes like our burgers.
We promise that you won't miss the mayo.*

Ingredients

1 lb medium red or golden potatoes, whole with the skin on

4 tbsp olive oil

2 tbsp apple cider vinegar

2 tsp mustard with horseradish

Pinch of salt and pepper

Preparation

Fill a medium pot halfway with cold water. Place potatoes in the water and bring to a boil. Once boiling, lower heat so the water is at a low boil. Cook potatoes until you can easily pierce them with a fork (about 20-25 minutes).

Drain the potatoes, and let them cool so they are cool enough to handle. Cut potatoes in quarters. In a bowl, whisk together olive oil, vinegar, and the mustard that has horseradish in it. Add potatoes and toss. Season with salt and pepper.

Serve hot or cold.

Quinoa with Zucchini

SERVES 4

*Let's face it; you can get tired of white rice. When we do, we switch to quinoa,
which is just as tasty and healthier for us anyway.*

Ingredients

2 cups water or vegetable broth

1 cup quinoa

1 zucchini, diced

Optional: grated Parmesan, red chili
pepper flakes

Preparation

In a small pot, add water or broth and quinoa. Bring
to a boil, and then reduce the heat to low to let this simmer. Cook for approximately 15 minutes and then add
the zucchini. Continue cooking for additional 5 minutes
or until all the liquid is absorbed. Remove from heat, cover, and allow to sit for a few minutes. Stir and serve hot,
topped with grated Parmesan or red chili pepper flakes.

Taylor's Tip
. . . .

*This recipe calls for
zucchini, but you can
add any steamable
vegetable you have
on hand—including
bell peppers, broccoli,
frozen peas, or corn.*

We love potatoes because they are tasty and we can make them so many different ways. But just remember to eat them before they sprout!

Baked

SERVES 1

Ingredients

1 Russet potato per person

Suggested toppings: butter, pepper, sour cream and chives, grated Parmesan cheese, bacon bits

Preparation

Pre-heat oven to 350 degrees. Wash the potato, dry it with a paper towel, and then wrap it in aluminum foil. Once the oven is heated, place the potato directly on the oven rack. Bake for approximately 1 hour or until soft when squeezed.

To prepare faster, put a few knife slits in the washed potato and cook it in microwave (without foil) on high for approximately 2 minutes. Remove from microwave, wrap in foil, and place on oven racks. Bake approximately 40 minutes.

Add toppings of your choice.

Boiled (Red or White)

SERVES 4

Ingredients

1-2 lbs white or red potatoes, unpeeled

Suggested toppings: butter, pepper, olive oil,
or grated Parmesan cheese

Preparation

Wash potatoes to remove any dirt. Place them in a medium pot filled 3/4 with cold water. Bring water to a boil, and lower the temperature to keep water at a low boil. Cook for approximately 20-25 minutes until "fork soft." Remove from heat, drain, and serve hot.

Add toppings of your choice.

Mashed

SERVES 6

Ingredients

1-2 lbs white potatoes

1/2 cup milk

3 tbsp butter

1/8 tsp salt

Suggested toppings: home-made gravy
(see recipe p. 130), pepper, butter

Preparation

Prepare the potatoes according to the instructions for boiled potatoes. After the potatoes are cooked and the water is drained, place them in a large bowl. Add 1/2 cup milk and 3 tbsp butter. Begin mashing with a potato masher or the back of a large fork, mixing the potato with the milk and melted butter. Sprinkle in 1/8 tsp salt. If the potatoes seem too dry, add additional milk.

Add toppings of your choice.

Easy Gravy

SERVES 4-6

What are mashed potatoes without gravy?

Ingredients

2 cups chicken broth

3 tbsp butter

3 tbsp flour

Pinch of salt and pepper

Preparation

Warm a medium skillet over medium-low heat. When warm, melt butter. Add flour and stir into a paste-like mixture. When lightly brown, add 1 cup of chicken broth and turn up the heat. Add salt and pepper. As the gravy thickens, you can add more broth if desired for yield or thickness. Turn the heat down and continue stirring until desired consistency is achieved. Adding additional chicken broth can help if sauce is too thick.

Serve hot over potatoes or roasted chicken.

Corn on the Cob

SERVES 4

There is nothing like an ear of corn at a summer picnic.
Who ever thought an ear could be so tasty?

Ingredients

4 ears of corn, shucked (1 ear per person)

Seasoned salt

Butter

Preparation

Fill a medium pot 3/4 of the way with water and bring to a boil. Add ears of corn and bring back to a boil. Once boiling, lower heat and simmer corn for approximately 3 minutes. Use fork to test if the kernels are tender and not hard.

Top with butter and seasoned salt.

Serve hot.

Taylor's Tip

· · · · · · · · · · · · · ·

"Shucking" corn means to pull off all the outer leaves and stringy silk that protect the kernels.

DESSERTS

19

We could try to say that our desserts include many important food groups, such as dairy, fruits, and vegetables. However, mostly, these recipes just call for some of our favorite dessert ingredients: chocolate chips, peanut butter, fudge topping, ice cream, and marshmallows. Of all of our desserts, you will have the most fun making our brownies since they are so fast to prepare and taste unbelievable.

Oatmeal Chocolate Chip Cookies

SERVES A SMALL GROUP

These cookies are pretty easy to make. However, if it's Finals Week and I don't have time, I can always count on my mom to send them to me.

Ingredients

2 sticks butter, softened (left on the counter for 1 hour)

1/2 cup brown sugar, packed (pushed into the measuring cup with a spoon)

1/2 cup white sugar

2 eggs

1-1/2 cups all purpose flour

1/2 tsp baking soda

2 tsp vanilla

2-1/2 cups old-fashioned oats

1 bag of chocolate chips

Preparation

Pre-heat oven to 325 degrees.

In large bowl, blend butter, brown sugar, and white sugar with a hand mixer on medium speed. Add in 1 egg at a time, continuing to beat with the hand mixer. Add vanilla and beat until everything is combined.

In a separate bowl, stir flour and baking soda together. Slowly add dry mixture to the butter and sugar mixture, blending on low until just blended. Then, with a large spoon, mix in oats and chocolate chips.

Using your hands, shape dough into balls 1 inch in diameter, and place on an ungreased cookie sheet. Make sure to leave a few inches of space between each ball.

Bake for approximately 12 minutes. Allow the cookies to cool slightly before removing them from the cookie sheet and serve.

Taylor's Tip

. . . .

To make classic chocolate chip cookies, you can leave out the oats and add 1/2 cup of flour.

Chocolate Peanut Butter Crisped Rice Squares

SERVES A SMALL GROUP

A variation to an old childhood favorite, we add peanut butter and chocolate chips to create a more updated dessert for college students. Besides, we always have one of our favorite cereals around and peanut butter and chocolate chips are never in short supply either.

Ingredients

6 cups of crisped rice cereal

1 (10 oz) bag of marshmallows (about 40)

1 stick of butter

1 cup chocolate chips

2 tbsp peanut butter

Preparation

In a large pot, melt the butter over medium-low heat. Stir in marshmallows and cook until melted. Add chocolate chips and peanut butter, and mix well. Stir in cereal until evenly coated with the marshmallow mixture. Scoop into a 4.8 qt glass dish, spreading evenly so the top is flat. Refrigerate until cool.

S'mores

SERVES A SMALL GROUP

Just because you aren't camping, doesn't mean you shouldn't get to enjoy the deliciousness that is s'mores. We eat them when we want to reminisce about being at home and having a campfire on the beach.

Ingredients

1 box of graham crackers

Bag of marshmallows

Chocolate bars

Preparation

If you have a gas stove, light one burner on medium heat. Place two marshmallows on a long roasting fork, and hold them over the flame until they turn golden brown. If you don't have a gas stovetop, you can heat the marshmallows above the electric grill for a minute or two.

Place the hot marshmallows and a piece of chocolate between two graham crackers to form a sandwich. Take a huge bite of your s'more!

Chocolate Pumpkin Brownies

SERVES A SMALL GROUP

*We make our brownies from a box, but change a couple ingredients to make
our brownies a little bit healthier and a little bit tastier.*

Ingredients

1 (15 oz) can of pumpkin purée (Libby's is a
popular brand.)

1 box of brownie mix

1 tbsp applesauce

Preparation

In a large bowl, mix together the three ingredients above. Scoop mixture into a lightly
buttered 8x8 or 2 qt glass baking dish. Then follow the baking instructions on the box to
cook the brownies. Allow for extra cooking time due to pumpkin mixture and for proper
cooling before cutting.

Apple Betty

SERVES 6-8

*This dessert is like an upside down apple pie for those days when
you aren't feeling right side up. It's another specialty of my grandmother's,
and she has passed it down to me.*

Ingredients

6 medium green apples, sliced

2 tbsp brown sugar

1 tbsp cinnamon

1 tbsp butter, cut into small bits

1 (11 oz) box of pie crust mix

1 tsp water

Optional: vanilla ice cream

Preparation

Pre-heat oven to 350 degrees.

In a small bowl, combine sliced apples, cinnamon, and 1 tbsp brown sugar.

Pour apple mixture into a small 8x8 or 2 qt glass baking dish. Top with bits of butter spread out over the top of the apples.

Combine 1/2 box pie crust mix, remaining 1 tbsp brown sugar, and 1 tsp water. Crumble mixture on top of apples. Bake for 40-45 minutes until the top is brown and the apples are bubbling.

Serve hot with vanilla ice cream or on its own.

Ice Cream Pie

SERVES 6-8

This recipe combines two of our favorite types of dessert into one very tasty, refreshing treat. It takes some time to make because of all the freezing, but you can use that time to catch up on studying or video games.

Ingredients

1 chocolate cookie pie crust

1 quart of your favorite ice cream, softened

1 (11 oz) jar of chocolate fudge topping

1 container whipped topping (such as Cool Whip), softened in the refrigerator

Preparation

Fill the bottom of the pie crust with a layer of fudge. Place in freezer and let freeze for an hour. It will not harden completely. Remove from freezer, and add ice cream in an even layer and freeze for approximately an hour until it hardens. Remove from freezer and cover the top with the remaining fudge. Freeze again for at least an hour. Remove from freezer and top with a layer of softened whipped topping.

Serve immediately.

BASIC SALAD
DRESSINGS

20

We usually buy these at the store for convenience—we can never get enough of Ranch dressing. However, for those who want to challenge themselves, we have included some basic, common dressings that are easy to make. Really. We're not kidding.

For each recipe, vigorously mix all the ingredients in a bowl or a salad dressing cylinder if you have one.

Caesar

YIELDS 2/3 CUP

3 oz olive oil

2 oz white wine vinegar

4 tsp Parmesan, grated

2 garlic cloves, minced

1 tsp anchovy paste

Pinch of black pepper

Vinaigrette

YIELDS 2/3 CUP

4 oz olive oil

2 oz apple cider vinegar or white wine vinegar

1 tbsp fresh lemon juice

1 tsp Dijon mustard

1/2 tsp black pepper

Balsamic Vinaigrette

YIELDS 1/3 CUP

6 tbsp olive oil

3 tbsp balsamic vinegar

1 tbsp fresh lemon juice

1 garlic clove, minced

1 tsp brown sugar

1/2 tsp black pepper

Pinch of salt

Ranch

1/2 cup mayonnaise

1/4 cup sour cream

1/8 cup milk

1/2 tsp onion powder or diced green onion

1/2 tsp garlic powder

Pinch of salt and pepper

Asian Vinaigrette

1/4 cup canola oil

1 tbsp soy sauce

2 tbsp rice vinegar

1/2 tsp sugar

Pinch of salt and pepper

DIPS AND SPREADS

21

1. Something Known, Something New

2. Cowboy Caviar

3. Salsa

4. Guacamole

5. Hummus

6. Aioli Spread

SOMETHING KNOWN, SOMETHING NEW

Some of these dips and spreads recipes are for foods you probably know, such as Salsa, Guacamole, and maybe Hummus. Two others, Cowboy Caviar and Aioli Spread, you may have never tasted. Give them all a try, and you will be pleasantly surprised.

Cowboy Caviar

SERVES A SMALL GROUP

Ingredients

1 cup of frozen corn

1 (16 oz) can black-eyed peas

2 avocados, chopped

2/3 cup cilantro, chopped

1/3 cup green onions, chopped

1/4 cup olive oil

1/4 cup red wine vinegar

2 garlic cloves, pressed or minced

1 tsp cumin

1/4 tsp salt

1/8 tsp pepper

Tortilla chips

Preparation

Mix all the corn, black-eyed peas, avocado, cilantro, and green onions in a bowl, and set aside.

In a separate bowl, mix the olive oil, red wine vinegar, garlic, cumin, salt, and pepper. Pour the resulting dressing over the corn mixture, and serve chilled with tortilla chips. Dressing should be added about 1 hour prior to serving.

Salsa

SERVES A SMALL GROUP

Ingredients

1 (14.5 oz) can of diced tomatoes

1 small jalapeno chili pepper, diced with seeds
(for medium-level hotness)

1/4 cup onion, diced

1 tbsp cilantro, chopped

1/2 tsp garlic powder

1/2 tsp chili powder

Pinch of salt

Preparation

Mix ingredients in a bowl and serve with your favorite tortilla chips.

Guacamole

SERVES A SMALL GROUP

Ingredients

3 avocados

1/4 cup salsa of your choice (recipe above)

1 tbsp fresh lemon juice

1/4 tsp garlic powder

Pinch of salt and pepper

Preparation

In a bowl, mash the avocado with a fork. Then mix in the remaining ingredients.
Serve with your favorite tortilla chips.

Hummus

SERVES A SMALL GROUP

Ingredients

1 (15 oz) can of garbanzo beans, drained and rinsed

1/2 cup olive oil

2 tbsp fresh lemon juice

2 garlic cloves, minced

1 tsp cumin

Optional: 1 tsp red chili pepper flakes

Preparation

Pulse all ingredients in a blender until smooth.

Good as dip for raw vegetables, or with pita bread. Also can be used as a spread for a vegetarian sandwich or as a salad dressing (toss well).

Aioli Spread

YIELDS ABOUT 1/2 CUP

Ingredients

1/2 cup mayonnaise or Greek style yogurt

3 cloves garlic, minced or pressed

1/4 tsp Dijon mustard

1 tsp fresh lemon juice

1 tsp fresh lime juice

1 tsp olive oil

Pinch of salt and pepper

Preparation

Vigorously mix all ingredients in a bowl until completely blended.

Good on our Pastrami Quesadilla and Ahi Sliders. Also can be used on sandwiches instead of plain mayonnaise.

SAUCES

22

WHEN YOU'RE HUNGRY

FOR HOME-MADE

These sauces can be used for any pasta. They can be store-bought for convenience, or can be made ahead of time and frozen for a quick, home-made meal.

Marinara Sauce

SERVES 6 - 8

Ingredients

3 tbsp olive oil

1 large onion, diced

2 garlic cloves, minced

2 (28 oz) cans crushed tomatoes

1 small (6 oz) can tomato paste

2 bay leaves

1/2 tsp sugar

Pinch of salt and pepper

Red chili pepper flakes

Optional: 1 tbsp oregano

Preparation

In a medium pot, warm olive oil on medium-low heat, and add onion and garlic. Sauté until onions are translucent. Add crushed tomatoes, tomato paste, sugar, bay leaves, red chili pepper flakes, salt, and pepper. Bring to a boil, and then lower heat and simmer for at least an hour.

Meat Sauce

SERVES 6-8

Sometimes called a Bolognese sauce, always tasty.

Ingredients

1 lb ground beef

1 large onion, diced

1 carrot, chopped

2 (28 oz) cans crushed tomatoes

1 small (6 oz) can tomato paste

2 garlic cloves, minced

3 tbsp olive oil

2 bay leaves

1/2 tsp sugar

Pinch of salt and pepper

Red chili pepper flakes

Preparation

In a medium pot, warm olive oil on medium-low heat. Add onion, carrot, and garlic. Sauté until onions are translucent. Add ground beef and simmer for approximately 5-7 minutes, breaking up the meat with a wooden spoon. Add crushed tomatoes, tomato paste, sugar, bay leaves, red chili pepper flakes, salt, and pepper. Bring to a boil, then lower heat and simmer for at least an hour. Don't eat the bay leaves!

Basil Pesto

SERVES 4

Ingredients

2 cups basil leaves, washed and patted dry

1/2 cup pine nuts or crushed walnuts

3/4 cup olive oil

2 garlic cloves, peeled

1/4 cup Parmesan cheese, grated

1/2 tsp lemon zest

Pinch of salt and pepper

Preparation

Add garlic, basil leaves, and pine nuts or walnuts to a blender. Slowly drizzle olive oil into the blender while pulsing the mixture. Add Parmesan cheese and lemon zest, and continue pulsing. If the sauce is too thick, drizzle in additional olive oil. Season with salt and pepper. Spoon mixture on pasta and toss.

Easy Cheese Sauce

SERVES 4

Good on chips for nachos or drizzled over vegetables

Ingredients

3 tbsp butter

3 tbsp flour

1-1/3 cups milk

2/3 cup cheddar or jack cheese

Preparation

In a small skillet, melt butter over medium-low heat. Stir in flour to create a paste. Slowly add the milk and continue stirring. Once all the milk is combined, slowly sprinkle in cheese until it is completely melted.

MARINADES

23

To flavor our dishes, we use soy sauce, olive oil, lemon, mustard, and a variety of spices. However, marinades are a great way to add extra flavor to meat and vegetables. The following marinades can be made at home or purchased at specialty markets like Cost Plus World Market.

For each recipe, vigorously mix all ingredients in a small bowl.

Chimichurri

YIELDS 3/4 CUP

Argentinian marinade used for chicken, pork, and beef.

Ingredients

1/2 cup olive oil

1/4 cup red wine vinegar

5 tbsp mix of parsley and cilantro, chopped

1 tbsp fresh lime juice

1 tbsp garlic, minced

1-1/2 tbsp dried oregano

2 tsp red chili pepper flakes

1 tsp black pepper

Pinch of salt

Piri Piri

YIELDS 3/4 CUP

Portuguese via Africa. Used for chicken and shell fish, such as shrimp.

Ingredients

1/2 cup olive oil

3 tsp red chili paste (Sambal Oelek is our choice.)

1/4 cup fresh lemon juice

2 tbsp cilantro, chopped

1 tbsp parsley, chopped

5 garlic cloves, minced

1/8 tsp salt

Honey Hot Sauce

YIELDS ABOUT 1/2 CUP

Good for chicken.

Ingredients

6 tbsp olive oil

3 tbsp white wine vinegar

1 tbsp hot sauce (We like Cholula.)

1 tsp honey

1 tsp garlic powder

1 tsp spicy mustard

1/2 tsp pepper

1/4 tsp salt

2 tbsp fresh lemon juice

Maple Syrup Ketchup

YIELDS ABOUT 1/2 CUP

Good for red meats.

Ingredients

6 tbsp olive oil

2 tbsp apple cider vinegar

2 tbsp ketchup

1 tbsp Worcestershire sauce

1 tsp maple syrup

1 tsp oregano

1 tsp garlic powder

1 tsp pepper

1/4 tsp salt

1 tbsp fresh lemon juice

24

SAMPLE MENUS

FINDING THE PIECES TO THE PUZZLE

You will find that our sample menus have been created to help you plan an entire dinner for friends, boyfriends or girlfriends. This is to encourage you to try different recipes from different food groups to organize a complete meal. In other words, the mystery of how everything "fits into the bigger picture" will be known to you. Your stomach will be happy for it too.

I. DATE NIGHT

Caesar Salad
(recipe p. 70)

Chicken Parmesan
(recipe p. 99)

Steamed Green Beans with Lemon and Olive Oil
(recipe p. 122)

Faux French Croissants with Ricotta Cheese and Chocolate Chips
Serve warm.
(recipe p. 44)

II. END OF FIRST SEMESTER DINNER

Mixed Green Salad
(recipe p. 69)

Roasted Chicken
(recipe p. 97)

Oven Roasted Veggies
(recipe p. 125)

Apple Betty
(recipe p. 138)

III. FALL TAILGATE

Game Day Chili
(recipe p. 78)

Corn on the Cob
(recipe p. 131)

Tailgate Sausage Sandwich
(recipe p. 64)

Nachos in a Bag
(recipe p. 117)

Oatmeal Chocolate Chip Cookies
(recipe p. 134)

IV. VALENTINE'S DAY DATE NIGHT

Tomato and Mozzarella Salad
(recipe p. 71)

Spicy Shrimp Pasta
(recipe p. 89)

Ice Cream Pie
(recipe p. 139)